MW01502852

Harry Would Be So Proud

A pocketful of funny and heartwarming stories

Eric V. Litsky

Eric V Litsky

ISBN: 9798777223821

Imprint: Independently published

Interior design: *The Writery Ink, LLC. Bloomfield, CT*

"I can only note that the past is beautiful because one never realizes an emotion at the time. It expands later, and thus we don't have complete emotions about the present, only about the past."

– Virginia Woolf

Eric V Litsky

For Norma

CONTENTS

With my grandmother, Minnie (Vernick) Sissman

and my big brother Andy.

Prologue

They named me *Vernick*.

What the hell were my parents thinking?

All my friends had normal, American middle names. Allen, Malcolm, Lewis, Benjamin, Sam and Ted. Then, of course, there was Samuel *Leonard* Rubinstein. I got stuck with *Vernick*. I hated it! I cringed when I had to share that nugget of information with friends. But it was a cultural thing. It was my grandmother Minnie's maiden name. Tradition prevailed on my parents. (Jews are funny that way.) The name marked me like an ugly birthmark.

At the mention of *Vernick*, I was teased, bullied, and laughed at. But, as the years passed, I began to appreciate the uniqueness of my middle name (not that middle names were used all that much). Mostly for official documents, a school registration card, or a driver's license, and of course, my Selective Service registration card which I referred to as '*my fucking draft card*'. I set fire to that card my first year in college, but that is a story for another day.

So, *Vernick* it was. *Eric Vernick Litsky*. A little pompous perhaps, but unique. And not without a little substance.

From my earliest memory, my grandmother was simply a sweet, grey-haired old lady. She was just a morsel of a woman, barely five feet tall in her sensible shoes. She and my grandfather lived in an attached home on White Plains Road in the east Bronx a couple of doors down from the elevated train that ran above Westchester Avenue. Every few minutes, a train going to or from Manhattan would rumble by. It was just loud enough to stop conversation for a moment as it shook the neatly displayed dishes in her breakfront cabinet. She kept a Kosher home which meant there were sets of dishes for meat and for dairy, as well as a third set for Passover. A lot of dishes rattled all day and well into the night.

Her tiny kitchen was scented with the aroma of chicken soup which she prepared by adding a small sprig of dill. That brought out the taste and lingered in the air like an overly perfumed woman who passed you on the sidewalk on a breezeless afternoon or was jammed next to you on the subway at rush hour.

On the shelf under her small kitchen window overlooking the Circle Movie Theater and the Westchester Avenue subway stop, was a snake plant called 'Mother-In-Law's Tongue' aptly named for its sharp, vertical leaves. Minnie had two sets of silverware: one for meat dishes and one for dairy. When I used the wrong fork or knife, which I did often, she snatched it up and placed it behind the plant. It seems the plant had a cleansing effect on the offending utensil.

If you looked through the leaves of that plant and out the window, you had a very narrow view of the world. Traffic, of course. An endless stream of commuters to and from the train. Kids playing stick ball. Occasionally a peddler, or the old man who rang a bell as he walked through the neighborhood to announce his presence. He sharpened knives and mended broken pots and pans. Minnie saw much more, but I'll come to that in a minute.

But what I remember most about Minnie's kitchen was a trivet in the center of her two-seat dinette table. It proclaimed in large, black metal letters, "No matter where I serve my guests, they seem to like my kitchen best." The woman could cook.

Each weekday morning, Minnie would wheel her shopping cart up White Plains Road to several independently owned, specialty food markets . . . the butcher shop, the bakery, the produce stand, and the fish market would each get its portion of Minnie's carefully budgeted food allowance.

My grandfather Louie had a one-man dental practice in the basement of their home. Though they lived a comfortable and secure life, he never forgot coming through Ellis Island as a poor Yiddish-speaking teenager. Remarkably, he did odd jobs at night to pay for his education. A year after graduating from dental school, the Stock Market crashed. My grandfather survived the Depression by working as a dentist for the NYC police department.

So, he watched their money carefully. Each week he would dole out a set amount of allowance for Minnie to buy groceries. She would shop ever so carefully, walking from store to store to get the best prices. She methodically saved nickels and dimes until they became dollars. She was a keen observer of society. Her view of the world was not limited by her narrow kitchen window.

In the 1930's when she saw more and more telephones being placed in homes, she bought stock in AT&T, Ma Bell. She foresaw the boom in grocery stores which put individual food markets under one roof. With cheaper prices and more convenience, she bought stock in A&P and Grand Union, the leading supermarkets of the day. In the late 1930's, construction on the Whitestone Bridge began. She foresaw that the connection between the Bronx and Queens would lead to the development of Queens and the rest of Long Island. She bought stock in the Long Island Lighting Company (LILCO), the electric utility. She was one smart cookie.

Many years later, when my grandfather discovered that she had parlayed her small savings into a respectable stock portfolio, he was speechless.

Minnie was born in the late 1890's in a small town just outside the city of Uman in the Ukraine, at the time a part of Russia. Her mother, Ida Vernick, was a single parent of three little girls. Abject poverty and frequent Cossack raids on their village forced her to look for a brighter future elsewhere.

Word had reached their little village that America was the land of opportunity where all could live safely and freely. So, with hope and enormous determination, she sold her belongings, packed up her three little girls and headed west. Eventually, she arrived in Liverpool, England, and booked passage on a NYC-bound White Star Line steamer for a new life.

The six-day passage in steerage, or third class, was horrible. Many passengers became ill and died. Out at sea, somewhere in the middle of the Atlantic, they were laid to rest in a watery grave halfway between the Old World and the new life they would never know.

As Ida set foot on Ellis Island with her three girls in tow, the joy soon turned to anxiety and the anxiety to near panic. She could demonstrate no means of support. She spoke no English and had no job skills. And her only family were her three girls under the age of six. The interviewer at Ellis Island believed that Ida and her three girls were sure to become a public charge, living out their lives on welfare. He unceremoniously stamped **DENIED** on her paperwork. The Vernick family was placed on the next steamer back to Liverpool. America simply did not want them.

The day after they docked back in Liverpool, Ida took a portion of her dwindling funds and once again booked steerage class passage to the New World. This time to Montreal.

She soon discovered the Canadians were more welcoming than the Americans and she was admitted. Ida was a gregarious woman, bright and energetic. She connected with a Jewish social service agency that would help her find a home and some part time work. But this home was to be temporary. Over the course of the next few months, she accumulated the funds needed to make her way to the predominantly Jewish neighborhood of the Lower East side of NYC. The 330-mile journey must have seemed to her a lifetime away.

Sometime in 1905, Ida, Minnie, Bess, and Rose entered the US as illegal aliens. Minnie spent much of her life worried about being deported. She eventually became a citizen and cast her first vote some 55 years after setting foot on American soil – for John F. Kennedy in 1960.

Ida worked wherever she was able, and the three girls enrolled in public school. Minnie finished her formal education some time in Junior High School when she joined many of her schoolmates sewing, cutting, and stitching in the sweatshops of the Garment District of lower Manhattan. The conditions were terrible. It was hot, cramped, and loud.

A short walk from the four-story cold water flat they lived in was the Triangle Shirtwaist Factory where a fire resulted in the deaths of 146 young women, including many of her friends. It kindled a movement and woke a rebellious spirit within her.

There were strikes against low wages, sexual harassment, and 12-hour workdays by teenagers called *"greenhorns."* And Minnie was right in the thick of it as an early member of the Ladies Garment Workers Union. She and thousands of other young Jewish women became outspoken supporters of not only the labor movement, but the suffrage movement as well.

Minnie Vernick - *fireball*. She organized strikes. Spoke at rallies. Walked picket lines. She risked everything for the downtrodden. She was arrested at a demonstration in New Jersey and was almost deported.

A bit later in life, she met a young man named Louie who was from a small town outside of Kiev. He spoke little English, but dreamed of becoming a doctor or perhaps a dentist in this new land. My grandparents made a life together living out their American Dream.

I never met my great grandmother, Ida Vernick. She died the year before I was born. It is said that she was a masterful card player, had a keen sense of humor, and was tough as nails when she needed to be. But she and my grandmother Minnie courageously blazed an oftentimes dangerous trail of twists and turns. And I am the last in my family to carry their name.

Yes, my middle name is *Vernick*.

Every story needs a beginning. Mine starts with these two incredibly strong women named Vernick......at the dawning of the 20th century.

As I looked down at enough lit birthday candles to set off a smoke alarm or melt the Carvel ice cream cake on which they sat, I thought about regrets. Sure, I've made lots of mistakes in my life and have done more than my share of stupid things. Those will be well documented with honesty and humor in the pages that follow.

I suppose if I had a 'do over' (a mulligan if you are a golfer), I would have flossed more often and spent much more time with my grandparents listening to their stories......about their times, about their lives. But like all youngsters, I was too busy being a kid.

Rarely does a young person have the patience or the curiosity to hear stories from older person's life. Having four grandchildren was all the encouragement I needed to write.

As I wrote I found I had more to talk about. And that my stories would entertain and be relevant to those of all ages and all walks of life. The details in the oral history of one's family fade over time. If nothing else, I hope that your reading of these stories not only entertain but encourage you to take your own pen to paper. And share the moments that shaped your life with the people you care about.

I believe that the greatest gift we have is not our collection of tchotchkes or other property. It is our stories. For who we are is the compilation of the stories of our lives.

Simsbury, CT

Keeping Your Word

The fifth grade at P.S. (Public School) 176 in Cambria Heights, Queens was not my favorite year. I was a 9-year-old who had not yet learned to read, but was clever enough to hide that fact from my teachers. And my parents.

I was an awkward kid. Girls scared me. And my face was beginning to break out. I sported a potbelly. A flat top crew cut. And could usually be found with a mouth full of bubble gum - fresh from a new package of baseball cards often found in my back pocket.

My teacher was Mrs. Lennon. Late in her career, she was overweight and overbearing. She didn't like me. I sat in the back of the classroom lost in my daydreams of the New York Yankees.

The Brooklyn Dodgers and New York Giants had recently left New York for California. If you were a baseball fan in New York, your only option was to root for the Yankees. The Mets would not show up for several years.

I was the middle child. Andy was two years older. He was bright and energetic. My little sister, Amy, was a pretty 4-year-old. Clearly the sparkle in my parent's eyes.

Did I mention that my mother was pregnant that year? This would be child number four in our increasingly crowded household. Like most housewives of the day, she stayed home to tend to our needs.

The new baby was due in late June.

My father was a NYC cop. He worked odd hours. When he was home, he was often asleep, trying to catch up after a night shift. We never knew when we could have friends over or make noise. So, we grew up playing in the schoolyard a few blocks away, in the streets, or at our friends' houses.

My dad offered to take me to my first big league game to celebrate my 10th birthday. He purchased tickets for June 30th a Friday night home game with the Washington Senators. For your baseball trivia file, The Washington Senators would soon relocate to become the Minnesota Twins, leaving our nation's capital without a baseball team until the Montreal Expos became the Washington Nationals in 2005.

For months, I watched every game I could. I listened to the night games on my transistor radio through an earpiece so as not to disturb my brother sleeping on the other side of the bedroom we shared.

Each day, I cut out and taped the previous day's box score and photos into a special Yankee scrapbook I kept. I knew all of the players and all of their statistics. This was very, very important to me.

The season wore on. The race to break Babe Ruth's single season home run record of 60 heated up between two Yankee sluggers. Mickey Mantle and Roger Maris.

Mickey was my guy. My hero. My father insisted on calling him Mickey Mantlepiece, a joke only he would laugh at.

On June 17, my new baby brother, Tommy, arrived. Eight days later was his bris, the traditional Jewish ritual of circumcising a baby boy. The event took place in our crowded basement with family and my parents' friends. I don't know what I found more disgusting, cutting the tip of my baby brother's penis or the chopped liver, pickled herring, and tongue sandwiches that accompanied the event.

I was raised in a Reform Jewish home, much less strict than the Kosher home of my grandparents. However, most traditional customs surrounding the birth of a child were observed.

It is the tradition that a baby is formally given its Hebrew name in the Synagogue at the first Friday night service available after its birth. It is the Hebrew name by which the child will be called in religious ceremonies throughout his life. The formal naming is an important and joyous occasion. It is the time for the entire Congregation, along with family and friends, to welcome the new child as a member of the Jewish people. All in all, it is a pretty big deal.

That date scheduled was June 30, 1961, the very evening my dad was to celebrate my 10th birthday at Yankee Stadium.

For the two weeks between my brother's birth and the date he was to be given his Hebrew name, enormous pressure was exerted on my father to cancel or reschedule our outing to Yankee Stadium. My parents fought about it. My grandparents stuck in their two cents, switching their argument from English to Yiddish when I entered the room. Even the Rabbi called my dad to lay on a little Jewish guilt. But my father was unrelenting.

He had made a promise. And when you give your *word*, you stand by it.

My father was never a baseball fan, but his word to me trumped a five-thousand-year-old Jewish ritual. And he withstood the pressure exerted on him. In short - he kept his word.

The night of June 30th was one I have never forgotten. As we walked through the tunnel under the stands to our section, the sounds from the crowd grew. And then I saw it in all its glory. The house that Ruth built. Yankee Stadium.

Up until then, my only experience of Yankee Stadium was what I could see on our small black and white Philco television. It sat on a swivel in the corner of our basement. It never occurred to me that the game and the Stadium would be in full color.

The perfectly mowed bright, green grass was surrounded by an eight-foot blue outfield wall. The white dental molding topped the upper deck stands. Some 60,000 fans cheered wildly when the Yankees took the field at the start of the game.

The game was spectacular. In the bottom of the sixth inning, Mickey Mantle smacked a ball to the deepest part of centerfield. As the ball banged around the outfield monuments (later enclosed), Mickey took off like a shot around the bases. He had struggled with bad knees his entire career. But not on this night. It was an inside the park home run, a rare feat, one which he would accomplish only 6 times in his 18-year, Hall of Fame career.

Whitey Ford, who pitched the Yankees to a victory that night, would go on to win the Cy Young award as the pitcher of the year. The baseball he would sign for me remains on a shelf in my office.

As memorable as my first professional baseball game at Yankee Stadium was, the gift my father gave me would impact my life and help to form the man I would become.

"If you give your word, even if it is to a 10-year-old boy, your word is your bond, a trust that must never be broken."

My dad lived a long life, well past his 90th year. Though we were very close, I don't think I ever properly thanked him for the life lesson he taught me.

First Kiss

It was 1961. The Cold War was in its adolescence and so was I.

The Soviet Union and the United States were testing increasingly more powerful nuclear weapons. Each nation stockpiled enough explosive power to blow up the world many times over. It was hard to wrap my 10-year-old brain around the end of the world.

Our answer to a nuclear attack was to direct school age children to take cover under their desks when the alarm sounded. This *'duck and cover'* drill was practiced over and over again. Like Pavlov's dog - when you heard the alarm, you ducked under the desk. I don't know how many times I hit my head on that wooden topped metal desk. I would stare aimlessly at the pieces of gum stuck to its underside until the *'all clear'* was sounded.

How they thought we could survive a nuclear blast hiding under a school desk was beyond me. But I had a more pressing, personal issue to deal with – Julie Greenberg. My first "crush."

I met Julie in the school yard. A pretty brunette. We talked once or twice that summer. I probably mumbled a lot, shifting from one foot to the other. I had no experience with girls, and I was profoundly shy. When the school year began, we found ourselves in the same 6th grade class. One day, she mentioned that she was going to have a house-party the day before Halloween. I was invited. It was going to be my first boy-girl party. And, drum roll please, my first time playing *'spin the bottle'*. Maybe, just maybe, I would get my first kiss. If the world ended after that kiss, so what!

A few weeks before Halloween, the Soviet Union placed missiles in Cuba capable of hitting major American cities. President Kennedy ordered a blockade of the island. He and the Soviet Premier were at a stalemate. The world held its collective breath as the deadline to remove the missiles from Cuba neared. We were on the verge of World War III.

It was all anyone could talk about. These *'duck and cover'* drills at school became a daily ritual. This was a terrifying time.

On Friday, October 26th an alarm once again sounded. This time, rather than ducking under our desks we were told to grab our jackets. The teachers marched us down the stairs to the basement fallout shelter, a place that they believed would withstand a significant blast. Several girls wept. Teachers became pale, their faces ashen. It was rumored that a couple of kids peed in their pants.

We huddled close together on the concrete basement floor. I pressed myself against the yellow block wall with my NY Yankee sateen jacket pulled over my head. There on the cold hard floor I was, left to wonder if I'd be blown to bits before ever getting my first kiss. After what seemed like an eternity, the *'all clear'* finally sounded. Slowly, we came back up the stairs, returning to our classrooms.

I expected to see our neighborhood looking like the aftermath of Hiroshima. Instead, traffic flowed. Houses were intact. Fall leaves blew about the windy streets. Everything was normal. Just another day in Cambria Heights. Yet something inside of me profoundly changed. For the first time in my short life, I seriously contemplated it coming to an end.

It was naturally assumed that 'ground zero' would be The Empire State Building. At the time, it was the tallest structure on earth. From the corner on 120th Ave. we could see the top of the building's spire once ascended by King Kong.

My dad told us that if a nuclear war ever were to come, we would simply go to the end of our street, hold hands and face the Empire State Building. Together we would watch the end of our world. It would be over in a matter of seconds. He was not a believer in fallout shelters and had no interest in trying to survive a post nuclear holocaust.

Then came Saturday. But due to the crisis, the boy-girl party was cancelled. There would be no *'spin the bottle'* for me. No Julie. No first kiss. I was devasted. The Cuban missile crisis would continue for a few more days. War was averted, and we were safe. But I had to wait for another year and for another girl to get my first kiss.

Four decades later, I see Julie across the ballroom at a neighborhood reunion. I take a long sip from my watered-down Bacardi and Coke and screw up the courage to walk over. I'm a grown man now with a family and a lifetime of experiences. Yet, the shy 10-year-old kid inside floats up to the surface.

I approach her as she is holding court with a cluster of old girlfriends. I overhear snippets of conversation of family. Careers. Successes. Typical reunion chatter. My mind wanders to a more innocent time. A simpler place. My old elementary school, PS 176.

PS 176 was large, encompassing two square city blocks. The two-story building overlooked a huge asphalt schoolyard with softball fields, basketball hoops and handball courts. It was the largest open area in Cambria Heights. And it was the center of activity for young people in the neighborhood.

The school was just a few blocks from our house, a red brick cape on 233rd Street, four houses off 120th Ave. My brother and I would walk to school and dash home for a quick lunch at noon each school day. It was a compact and densely populated neighborhood full of small, single family brick houses.

The schoolyard is where I learned how to play sports and make friends. It is where I negotiated the complexities of pre-teen life. It is where I hit my first home run, a hard ground ball through the legs of the second baseman that rolled all the way to the basketball courts. And it is where I had my first fight, a brawl that lasted all of 10 seconds but was talked about for weeks. I lost.

And it is where I met Julie, who half a lifetime later is standing a few feet from me. Her conversation ends and I step in and introduce myself. She looks at my face and then my name tag, offering no sense of recognition.

I reminded her that we were in the 6th grade together. We chatted for a few minutes. I wished her well. And I gave her a kiss.

Lost and Found

I was four. Lost in the largest city in America.

When my dad had a Saturday off, something special would be planned. My family loved to take advantage of all that NYC had to offer.

We once took the Ferry from lower Manhattan to the lesser known of the five NYC boroughs, Staten Island. We sailed pass the Statue of Liberty and the new Verrazano Bridge, which is the world's, longest. Back in Manhattan, we had lunch in Chinatown. I thought the boat ride had brought us to China. Don't laugh at me. I was little. Other trips took us to the Bronx Zoo. Museums. Coney Island. The Empire State Building. And Central Park.

One summer day, my parents took my brother and me to The Museum of Natural History. I was 4 years old. We were joined by their friends and their two children.

Four adults. With four children. What could go wrong?

I vividly remember being in awe of the massive displays of dinosaurs in the museum. And falling fast asleep in its Hayden Planetarium. Under a billion stars. It was a fun day! We gathered at the exit doors and headed out to grab some food. Within a block, they lost me.

They walked down Columbus Ave. I took a right on Amsterdam Avenue in a very busy upper Westside neighborhood. I was four.

And *they* were lost in the largest city in the world.

I wandered into an Italian deli. The owners were an older couple with a slew of kids. They sat me on an orange crate in their big display window looking out at a parade of people passing by on the wide sidewalk.

I remember the mom the clearest. She was a big woman with a warm smile and a bit of a moustache. She had a sweet reassuring voice. She told me not to worry. She would take care of me until my parents showed up. I looked around the store. Lots of food. New kids to play with. Okay to me. I was not upset or afraid.

She gently told me to look out to the street for my parents. They would soon be walking by. Worried that I was misplaced, she never said the word "lost." And I didn't know what misplaced meant.

After a while, she gave me a pear to eat. I had never seen a pear before. It was a new shape and new taste. The juice ran down my face. It was delicious. Sometime later, I saw my parents walking down the street looking for me. I knocked on the window. A happy ending to what might have become a truly traumatic story.

Some 40 years later, I found myself back in that very neighborhood, across the street from the Beacon Theater. The deli was still there. I had hoped that it would be operated by the same family. What a heartwarming story I would have shared with them.

But that was not to be. The old Italian deli was now a Korean market, run by a nice couple with a slew of kids of their own. I shrugged my shoulders, smiled to myself, and bought a pear.

It was the second-best pear I ever ate.

It Ain't Frosty, Kid

Everyone in the theater screamed. Or maybe it was just me. I couldn't stop screaming. That was my first trip to the movies, *sans* parents. I was 6 years old. One Saturday morning, a dozen kids from my neighborhood went to the movies, by ourselves and unescorted. You gotta love the 1950s.

We walked three blocks up 233rd street to Linden Boulevard where we caught the Q-4 bus. It was a mile bus ride to the Cambria Heights Movie Theater.

The leader of our group was Kenny. He lived a few doors from us. He was 10, the big kid on our street and he was in charge. Why he was the one put in charge, I'll never know. He was the idiot who rode his Schwinn bike into our 12' round backyard pool. It collapsed sending two thousand gallons of water pouring down our driveway onto the street, some into our next-door neighbor's basement. But he was the tallest. And the oldest. So, we had to listen to him.

This was our first outing with no adult supervision. We put our coins in the coin box adjacent to the bus driver and took our seats. What an exciting journey this was for us. A one-mile trip on the bus when you are six is like travelling to the other side of the world. I stared out the window, looking at the shops I had never seen. Ten stops later, we pulled the cord, ringing the chime to let the driver know we were getting off at the next stop. Each of us took a turn pulling on the cord, clearly annoying the driver and the other passengers on the bus.

There it was in front of us. A gigantic Marquee announcing the feature movie of the day: "The Abominable Snowman," starring Forrest Tucker and Peter Cushing. I had been to the movies a couple of times before with my parents, but I was little and didn't remember those experiences very well.

This was going to be great. I assumed Abominable was another name for Frosty. And that we were seeing a new version of the animated feature *"Frosty, the Snowman."* No one told me different.

Kenny handled the admission tickets. He handed them to a guy dressed in a blue vest and a weird hat. If memory serves, it was a fez. Before finding our seats, we lined up at the candy counter. I bought a small box of popcorn with extra butter so I could lick my fingers. My brother Andy helped me complete that transaction. I didn't know how to make 30 cents out of the nickels and dimes I had in my pocket. Don't laugh at me. I was 6.

We took our seats, almost filling an entire row, and settled in for a treat. The lights dimmed. A couple of cartoons played followed by an episode of the old serial *"Buck Rogers."*

Then the feature film began. Halfway through the movie, about the time I finished my popcorn, I realized that Frosty wasn't coming. There was some creature out there in a Tibetan Mountain range killing these people.

"Where the hell was Frosty?"

The one scene that remains etched in my memory bank forever is when the Yeti reaches his hairy, clawed hand under the tent where the lead characters are sleeping. Everyone in the theater screamed. Or maybe it was just me. I couldn't stop screaming.

I have slept in many tents over my lifetime. I was a boy scout. Camping was a cheap getaway when I was in college. And I took my kids tent camping when they were young.

But I have not spent one night without putting something between me and the side of the tent to protect me from my vivid memory of the hairy, clawed hand of the *"Abominable Snowman."* It scared the shit out of me at six years old. And it still does. Where the hell was Frosty when I needed him?

Bite the Bullet

What a nightmare. Mrs. May, my second-grade teacher at PS 176, was a horror show. She was mean and looked a little like the witch in "Hansel and Gretel."

Each Friday afternoon, we had a spelling bee – words taken from the vocabulary list we had worked on during the week. Small clusters of students would compete by spelling the words on the blackboard at the front of the room. Spelling was not and is still not my forte. And it is nerve-wracking at any age to write on a blackboard in front of a full classroom.

The word that got me into trouble was **SHIRT**. I spelled it without the R. Yes, in my best handwriting I wrote the word *Shit* in large letters on the blackboard at the front of the class.

Mrs. May was furious with me. She lost it and smacked me on the back of the hand with a ruler. It was all I could do to keep from crying, which in a NY minute would have ruined my elementary school career. Of course, I was oblivious to my spelling error. I hid the small welt on my hand from my parents. It healed. Life in the second grade went on.

The next Saturday morning I *accidentally* threw a rock, breaking one of the panes in our gigantic classroom window. Come on. I was 7. Besides, no one saw me.

Sometime in the fall, a note was sent home inviting dads to come in to share what they did for their work. It was the 1950s. Women rarely worked outside of the home. My mother was a homemaker.

My dad was a NYC policeman.

My dad's work hours were unpredictable. He rotated through different shifts, sometimes working all night and sleeping all day one week, then reversed the next. We were never sure when he'd be home or whether he'd be awake or asleep.

As it turned out, he was available to visit my classroom on the specified day. He seemed excited. I didn't really care one way or the other.

He and two other fathers signed up for their 5-minute spiel. We returned from recess that day to see the three dads up at the front of the room. Cambria Heights was a working-class neighborhood. Most of the men worked in some capacity for the city. I can't remember what the other dads did for a living, but I couldn't take my eyes of my father.

My dad came into the classroom in full dress uniform, a holstered .38 caliber handgun with a belt full of bullets, white gloves and a shiny badge, and his recently acquired Sargent's stripes on each sleeve. He looked like a god sitting up there at the front of our classroom. Everyone was awestruck. Even Mrs. May was impressed. My stock in my second-grade class increased dramatically.

The first two fathers babbled on about what they did for a living. And then Mrs. May introduced Sargent Litsky, Eric's dad. He was spectacular.

As he talked about riding in his squad car, arresting bad guys. And keeping his precinct safe. I sat up tall in my seat. Just as proud as any 7-year-old could possibly be of his dad. The coup de grace was when we took a bullet out of his holster and had the kids pass it around the room. I was about to burst I was so excited. It could not have been a better moment. It was perfect.

And then he asked if there were any questions.

One of my classmates asked if he ever shot his gun. My dad answered in cop language. Everyone was sitting on the front edge of their seats.

> *"My partner and I pulled our squad car up to a grocery store that was in the process of being burgled* (he could have said robbed*). The alarms were going off. I sent my partner around to the rear of the building. And I went in through the broken front door. We both had our guns drawn. We called for backup."*

There was an audible "Wow" from my classmates. I had never heard this story.

Dad continued:

> *"I opened the door in search of the perpetrator* (he could have said bad guy*) and found myself face to face with a ferocious guard dog. I could not get past it. Having no other option, I shot the dog."*

The was a moment of silence. Then some wise ass a few seats behind me said, *"Hey Eric, your dad shot Lassie."*

In that moment, all the air escaped from my pumped-up little chest. I shrank lower and lower into my chair. Several kids giggled. I think I even saw that nasty Mrs. May smirk a bit, reclaiming her classroom power.

He finished up his story, but I had stopped paying attention. Frankly, I don't know how it ended. My moment of high status came and went…. at the speed of a bullet. I learned that day that you don't gain status by the accomplishments of others. **Respect is individually earned.**

The other lesson I learned was how to spell S-H-I-T.

My Public-School Education

A couple of hours after setting foot in a school for the very first time. I was grabbed by my ear, shoved back into a chair, and screamed at by a hysterical teacher.

I attended a 2-week summer program with the neighborhood kids. I was in preschool, getting ready for kindergarten. I'm not sure how one gets ready for kindergarten. I think you just show up and try not to shit your pants.

Up till then, my only experience with school was watching the Little Rascals on TV. I looked a little like Spanky. I was short and round, sporting a pair of adult-sized ears. Needless to say, *"Dumbo"* was not my favorite Disney movie.

When the Rascals finished their school day, Spanky would give a big wave to his teacher, Miss Crabtree, and say, *"So long, Toots."* She would smile. Spanky would smile. And there was joy.

As we walked out of the classroom for recess that very first day, I gave my teacher a big wave. And said in my cutest little voice, *"So long, Toots."* This did not go over well. She grabbed me by my most prominent feature, my enormous left ear. And vigorously hauled me back into the classroom.

"Don't toots me," she yelled at the top of her lungs. *"Toots me once more and I'll knock your teeth down your throat."*

Not the Miss Crabtree response I had anticipated.

She went on to scream at me for the next 30 minutes until recess was over. I don't remember crying. I think that enraged her even more. I just sat there wondering what the hell I did wrong. The remaining days in that summer program were a blur. I just stayed out of this crazy lady's way. And I never 'tootsed' anyone ever again.

I learned to live with my out-sized ears. But I was also severely pigeon toed, my feet turning oddly inward. My parents had me fitted with corrective inserts. Now my oversized shoes made my feet look as out of place as my ears. I was quite a sight. All I needed was a 'kick me' sign on my back.

One morning walking to school - I was in kindergarten and my brother Andy was in the 2nd grade - some big kids started to pick on us. They were huge. And old. Might have been 4th or 5th graders. I didn't know what to do or how to handle the situation. So, I kicked one of them in the balls. Pretty hard. With my heavy oversized shoe.

From that day forward, they called me "The professional kicker." I had no idea what that meant. I was in kindergarten. But I was never bullied again.

Except for these events and the three earlier stories (Bite the Bullet, Keeping Your Word, and First Kiss). My elementary school years went by largely without incident.

But I did have a secret. I could barely read.

As the 6th grade was winding down, we received our class assignments at JHS 59, which we would attend in the fall. JHS 59 was a 4-story building with over a thousand 7th and 8th graders. A 15-minute bus ride from our house.

There were over 20 classes in each grade, arranged from the most challenging to the least challenging. Classes 7-1 to 7-6, were the college bound track with foreign languages and arts enrichment programs.

Classes 7-7 to 7-15 ran on a much slower track, prepping its students with hopes of graduating from high school. The classes from 7-16 and higher were populated with students with a myriad of disabilities. Learning. Behavioral. Emotional. Physical. Students referred to it as the "Prison Track."

My pre-placement at JHS 59 was in class 7-16. Though my test scores showed math abilities at a high school level, I could barely read at a 3rd grade level.

While you can't argue with a standardized test, you can retake it.

So, in the summer before entering Junior High, I was enrolled in a special program to improve my reading skills and learn how to successfully take a standardized test. Each weekday morning, I'd take a half hour bus ride to Hillside Ave in Jamaica. I'd then walk about eight blocks to a street front office where I'd spend the next three hours learning how to read.

When summer ended, I retook the placement exam and was placed in 7-2. A fresh new start.

This was an exciting time. The Beatles topped the charts and made their first visit to America. The NY World's Fair opened in nearby Flushing Meadows. And the Kennedys brought new energy to the White House. They called it Camelot.

One November afternoon, the principal announced over the loudspeaker system that the President had been shot. My first thought was that somebody shot Steven Chang, the president of our student government. It took a while to sink in. It was President Kennedy who had been assassinated.

I didn't understand the significance of the moment until seeing the faces of the teachers and administrators. They were stunned, many brought to tears. Everything I knew and could count on was about to change. I just did not grasp at that time how much.

We each muddled through the grim November days that followed. But there was no emotional support system. No way deal with the shock that would last well into our adult years.

I think that the combination of the Cuban Missile Crisis and the Kennedy assassination birthed an energy among baby boomers that would fill the decade with drugs, sex, Rock and Roll, and rebellion.

Meanwhile. We looked forward to moving on to high school. As we rehearsed our commencement ceremonies, the principal spoke words I have never forgotten.

> *"For many of you, this will be your <u>only</u> graduation. So, it is important for you and your families that you are well behaved. Please take this ceremony seriously."*

Talk about setting a low bar.

At that time, the NYC school system offered admission to three very competitive high schools. Stuyvesant High School, Bronx High School of Science, and Brooklyn Tech. A standardized test was given to 8th graders. Two summers earlier, I had learned how to take a standardized test. That lesson paid off. I was admitted to Brooklyn Tech.

My family was so excited. I gained admission to one of the best public high schools in the country. But no one ever anticipated how horrible the experience would be for me.

Brooklyn Tech is a 9-story building with over 7,000 boys. Yup. At the time, girls were not offered admission. The area around the school - now full of multi-million-dollar brownstones - was largely comprised of burnt out and abandoned buildings. Broken windows and graffiti were everywhere.

It was a rough neighborhood. We joked that our track team owed its success to training across the street at Fort Greene Park. Slow runners wouldn't make it out alive. One bus and two trains. My commute began at 6:30 am. It was a little under two hours each way to get to school. I was fourteen years old. And miserable.

Towards the end of the first semester, the NYC subway system went on strike. It was an act of God. My saving grace. I could no longer get to Brooklyn. I was forced to attend the local high school with my friends. Due to the overcrowding, the school was on double sessions. My school day now began at 10am. Finally, some sleep.

Even better. BOOBS!!!

Andrew Jackson High School had girls. Within days, I permanently transferred. Life got much better.

Andrew Jackson High School was an urban high school with some 4,000 students. Much less intense than Brooklyn Tech, but still crowded and loud. It was a solidly integrated school with roughly the same number of students of color as white students. Everyone got along just fine.

After the assassinations of Malcom X, Martin Luther King Jr., and Bobbie Kennedy, the Black Power movement took hold. There was noticeable racial stress. Black students were finding a new footing, establishing a new identity. I respected that then as I do today.

In my senior year, fights broke out, unfortunately, along racial lines. Exaggerated media reports inflamed the situation. The principal called together student leaders, faculty, and administrators to discuss the issue. I was a member of the student body council, so I had a seat at the table.

Joining us was Congressman James Scheuer, a recently announced candidate for Mayor of NYC. As we went around the room introducing ourselves, you could have heard a pin drop when he smacked the conference room table. In his booming voice said:

"Eric Litsky. How have you been? It's been a while. You look great."

"Fine sir," I replied.

"Why don't you come visit. I'm sure Laurie would love to see you," he added.

The meeting went on for a while with everyone speaking in platitudes accomplishing nothing. The local paper snapped some photos. That was the end of it.

The question remained, however: How did a kid from Cambria Heights have such a friendly relationship with a 13-term Congressman from the Bronx? I wasn't about to tell them.

The truth is that the previous summer I worked with the American Jewish Society for Service, an anti-poverty program in Lackawanna, NY, just outside of Buffalo. The Congressman's daughter was in the same program. We had bit of a summer romance.

The meeting broke up. Congressman's aide asked me if I would help organize Students for Scheuer in his bid to become the next Mayor of New York. I agreed.

The campaign asked me to do some advance work for him in Jamaica that weekend. I was to walk down crowded Hillside Ave handing out flyers in my loudest voice inviting people to *"Meet the next Mayor of NYC."*

Eight blocks later I turned around. He had given up and went home. Nobody told me.

I noticed that I had stopped walking in front of the very storefront from where I had spent my summer mornings as a 12-year-old learning to read. A small world indeed. Frustrated with my first campaign experience, I tossed the remaining flyers in the ubiquitous silver metal trash can. My interest in political campaigning abruptly ended.

The Congressman finished dead last in the Democratic Primary.

My first-grade class. I'm seated behind the desk 2nd from the left (note the big ears).

Harry Would Be So Proud

He was a middle-aged Black man who drank and smoked too much. I was eight years old, and he was my friend. Outside of my immediate family and a couple of close friends, there was one constant in my life from early childhood until I left home for college. His name was Harry.

Harry cleaned our house every Friday before my grandparents arrived for their weekly visit.

Harry was the only Black person I knew. Cambria Heights at that time was virtually all-white. The only diversity was among Jews, Italians, and Irish. That would soon change as our neighborhood and schools were gradually integrated.

I would soon spend my childhood summers in multi-ethnic summer camps run by various Settlement Houses based on the Lower East Side of Manhattan. That would be my first true exposure to diversity – where my buddies were for the most part Black, and my summer girlfriends Black or Puerto Rican.

The undercurrents of race relations ran tangentially through my young life. These were the 1950s and early 1960s. As our neighborhood became more integrated, predatory real estate agents tried to create panic selling….'white flight.' Block busting. My father and a friend went door to door convincing neighbors not to panic and that this great neighborhood would be even better as it became more integrated. And it was.

Even at a young age, I was aware and proud of my father's actions. This was a great place to live.

But for me, I looked forward to coming home from school on Fridays and chatting with my friend Harry. We'd talk sports. And about school and girls. Tears welled up in his eyes one day when he shared that his sister had recently died. He said he was very sad. It was a very awkward moment for a boy not yet 10. I just told him that I was sorry for that.

I once shared with him that I was getting picked on in school by a bully. He showed me how to make a proper fist – thumb outside on top of the other four fingers.

"Ball up your fists. Look him straight in the eye and tell him to back off or you'll punch him in the face. They almost always back off."

"What if they don't," I asked?

"Every so often you get your ass kicked," he added. "Just hang on and someone will break it up."

Harry was a sweet man. A gentle soul. A church-going man. He was happy cleaning up after our family of six. On Fridays, our small house smelled of Mr. Clean, Parliament cigarettes, and whatever he happened to be drinking that day. More often than not, gin.

Harry was an alcoholic. By late afternoon, he was almost always three sheets to the wind. Alcoholism was not something we had any experience with, so we ignored it. And to our shame, were entertained by it.

One afternoon, Harry was in a terrible fight with my brother Tom's inflatable Popeye punching bag. Each time Harry punched it, Popeye would pop back up. Harry would hit it again. Sensing that this was more than a fair fight, I backed out of the room and left them battling.

Harry would stack our stuff in neat piles. I peeked in on him once as he was returning my sister Amy's dolls to their rightful place on the shelf in her room. He shared brief comments to each of her dolls.

I smiled.

My mother once had the executive board of the PTA over for a meeting on a Friday afternoon. Harry had left an empty bottle of Thunderbird (very cheap fortified wine) in the waste basket. It did not go unseen by the good ladies of Cambria Heights. There was gossip.

Periodically, he would get into my father's bar. One Friday, he replaced the vodka with water. Sometime later, my father mixed a screwdriver (vodka and orange juice) for a guest. He fired Harry.

After a few weeks, my mother would convince my father that Harry had learned his lesson. Harry would be rehired with a stern lecture. He promised he would not touch my father's liquor. My dad would rarely drink, but he took a lot of pride in his bar with neatly arranged bottles of every shape and size.

Had my dad not become a cop, he might have made a pretty good bartender. He liked to listen to other people's problems. His bottles were dusted, and when carefully placed on his bar, there was order in his life. My siblings and I would often salute the bottles on his bar. Or the cans in the kitchen cabinet. Or the books on his bookshelf as each stood crisply at attention.

When my dad became a lieutenant in the NYPD, he received a special gift from a dear friend: a bottle of Haig & Haig Pinch, an expensive whiskey in a unique triangular bottle.

Through the years, my brother Andy and I got caught doing a lot of stuff we shouldn't. Dad would get pissed off, but he never completely lost it. When Harry got into his Pinch, I thought he was going to put him through the wall. Harry was fired. This time for a month.

My Bar Mitzvah party took place in our finished basement. Harry, who had been rehired for some time by then, helped my mother with the set up. He was also a guest. My guest. As the music echoed up the stairs, my dad saw Harry dancing. He invited him to come down to join the party. Harry just stood there with a great big smile.

And his baritone voice boomed out "I am so proud."

From that day forward when something special happened to any of us in the family, we would honor this good man's memory by saying, "Harry would be so proud."

The Bad Penny

My brother Andy and I fought over just about everything. We had different friends, different interests. He was two years older and thought he was smarter. (Which he was, but I was too stubborn to admit it).

To keep us from our nightly squabble - who controlled the television, my parents devised an ingenious system. On even numbered days, Andy would pick the tv shows while I would have to clear dinner dishes and vacuum the floor. On odd numbered days, I'd get the tv. Andy would clean up after dinner. My parents could relax while one of us cleaned up with no more dinner time fights to referee except for those months that had thirty-one days.

Andy and I shared a bedroom in our small home in Cambria Heights. To keep his stuff away from my stuff, we ran a piece of masking tape through the center of the room. The door to our room was a little off center. I had to hop to get in and out so as not to set foot on his side of the room.

We both had an interest in coin collecting. I liked to put pennies and nickels in my blue tri-fold coin album. He preferred more exotic coins: Indian Head pennies, Buffalo Nickels, a Morgan silver dollar when he could afford it. We were both well aware that the rarest and most valuable penny was the 1909 S VDB.

The penny was designed by the sculptor Victor David Brenner whose initials VDB appeared on the rear of the coin. Very few were struck by the mint in San Francisco, designated by the *S* under the date on the front of the coin.

It was rare and valuable. Worth twice the value of our house.

Long story short, we found a very worn-down penny. We thought it was the incredibly rare and valuable 1909 S VDB penny. Of course, we both claimed ownership to it. Either he found it on my side of the room, or I found it on his side of the room.

When my parents came home from an evening out, every light in the house was on. Andy and I were screaming at each other. I was 8. He was 10. Or there surely would have been F-bombs thrown.

I said, "I think you're an ass fart."

He screamed back, "I think you're a little shit."

My parents separated us and looked more closely at the coin in question.

This was an old penny. Pretty worn down. It was hard to read the date, the S, or the VDB designation since we did not have a good magnifying glass. We agreed to table our battle until Friday when my grandparents would come for dinner. My grandfather was a dentist and he had a very large magnifying glass.

For the next two days, I dreamed of box seats at a ballgame. Andy dreamed of getting on an airplane and travelling far away. My parents dreamed of moving to a larger home…. or maybe sending us to military school.

Friday came. Before my grandfather could take off his suit jacket, we were pulling at him. Under the brightest light in the house above the kitchen table, he carefully inspected the coin with his gigantic magnifying glass. He looked on one side. Then the other. I wanted to scream for him to hurry up, but this was a man who took his time with important matters.

Finally, after several minutes there was no longer a dispute. The coin was a 1909 S. But the VDB initials on the back was nothing more than a scratch. We quickly pulled out our coin book to determine its value. And learned that the coin in very good condition - which this was not - was worth.... THIRTEEN CENTS.

Just like that our dreams burst.

Today, when I hear the expression *"a penny for your thoughts,"* I smile to myself and think about our penny; the penny that was not to be. Many years later, I got to sit in box seats at the ballgame. Andy has since traveled the world. And my parents eventually bought a larger home to live out the last 30 years of their lives. All without the benefit of an outrageously expensive coin.

All things in their own time.

A penny for your thoughts?

Grounded

The steel monster stood 262 feet, the height of a 24-story building. Strapped onto canvas seats, we were pulled slowly to the top by a steel cable. It took a little over a minute to reach the release point. The Coney Island Parachute Jump, Brooklyn's Eiffel Tower. I told my brother Andy I thought I could see across the ocean to France. He told me to shut up. We both held on to the straps tight enough for our little fingers to turn white.

The fifteen seconds to float down to earth were terrifying. We landed with a bounce. For a moment, I thought something broke and that we were going to die. I'm pretty sure a few drops of urine discolored my white jockey shorts.

That's how fast it happened. Mid-way through elementary school, I developed a lifelong fear of heights. Prior to that, I was a champ at climbing the monkey bars in the school yard behind P.S. 176. I could hang upside down from the top wrung, swinging from bar to bar until my white Keds safely touched down on the black asphalt below.

We would climb the crabapple tree in our backyard, shimmy up the old tree in no time flat. At the highest branch, we could peek over the top of our house and see the spire of the Empire State Building six miles away in Manhattan. We were on top of the world. But, after one scary parachute ride, the damage was done. From that moment on, I was scared shitless of heights. As the years passed, I tried to not let my fear of high places get the better of me. I've not been successful.

I once took a date to Six Flags. I thought I could win her a teddy bear on the Midway. I knew the trick to shooting out the star with the little machine gun, but she wanted to ride the Ferris Wheel. So up we went in an open-air car, no safety belts, and a lot of air between us and the ground. By the time we reached top, I was sitting on the floor of the car, my arms and legs hugging the metal support bar. Not my manliest moment. She patted my back, soothingly telling me that it would be OK. That was a first and last date.

I once attempted to stroll down the Bright Angel trail at the Grand Canyon. A few minutes in and I was taking side to side baby steps back as I hugged the canyon wall. A similar fate met me on the Inca Trail at Machu Picchu in the Peruvian Andes. And on top of Haleakala on Maui.

Early in our relationship, my wife Norma and I took a hot air balloon ride on a trip out west. The basket was scalloped with the corners curved upward to the height of about four feet. I planted myself in one of the corners and hung on. Silently, we rose above the desert floor. As the views became more and more spectacular, my legs became more and more wobbly.

I reached for Norma and held her close. I told her she was my anchor. She thought I was being so romantic, but I was being literal. Hanging on to her for dear life. We survived. I don't care for hot air balloons, but I still have Norma to hang on to.

She remains my anchor.

Home Cooking

There was the time that my grandmother nearly killed my entire family. She took a half-cooked brisket to Brooklyn for my cousin Matthew's bris. It was an hour ride from The Bronx on an unair-conditioned subway. Her plan was to finish cooking the brisket when she got there. Science had other ideas. It nearly wiped out three generations of our family in a single July afternoon.

Other than her 'killer brisket,' my grandmother was a pretty good cook. When I ate at her home, I didn't get a pain in the center of my chest like when I ate my mother's cooking. Only a Rolaids could soothe that pain. But when I close my eyes and visualize my grandmother's tiny kitchen, it is her chicken soup that still fills my senses.

She cooked simply. Boring by today's 'foodie' standards. Her favorite and perhaps her only spice was salt. She salted everything! That might have been a Jewish thing in those days. It also might explain why everyone in my family takes medication to control their blood pressure.

When I find myself at less than my best, I look for Grandma's simple comfort foods: Cottage cheese over cling peaches fresh from the can, or with a bowl of flat noodles. Admittedly, it is *spiceless*. And for the most part *tasteless*. But it is like a hug from my grandma. And who doesn't want a hug from Grandma when you are feeling under the weather. Meals in my childhood home would not have delighted anyone's gastronomic senses. The center of our small house was the kitchen. There was a wall phone with a cord long enough to walk through most of the house. Next to the phone where the listings of emergency numbers, fire, police ambulance, etc. would normally be where the numbers of restaurants that delivered. Chang's Chinese. Chicken Delight. Tosca's Pizza. And my particular favorite, Jim's Deli where we could get delicious deli sandwiches of all varieties.

It wasn't all takeout meals. My mother would sometimes cook. When she was in the mood, she would burn the protein du jour. Though we were a middle-class family of six on a cop's salary, we did eat some variety of meat almost every day. I recall that lambchops were made edible by drowning them with large dollops of apple sauce. And those burnt little disks we referred to as hamburgers, had a lot of crunches to them. They required a copious amount of ketchup and a side of baked beans.

But the show stealer was her chicken. My mother would remove the plastic wrap from the frozen chicken. Unable to separate the Styrofoam, she'd just start cooking. After several minutes in the oven, it would defrost enough so she could peel the Styrofoam from the still frozen chicken.

We survived.

My mother's spice rack was mainly for show. She only used two spices. Salt, of course. And Paprika on every poultry dish she burned.

Our favorite lunch treat growing up was pizza. Not the amazing NYC pizza. You know, the slice that you had to fold to eat. It burned the roof of your mouth as the hot oils ran down the inside of your wrist. No, this was Betty's (my mom's) pizza. A melted slice of Kraft American cheese covering a well toasted Thomas's English muffin, topped by a spoonful of Ragu Spaghetti Sauce or ketchup if we were sans sauce.

It might surprise you to learn that the four of us who survived my mother's cooking have become very good cooks, though none of us follow recipes particularly well. We cook by instinct. There is joy in the process. For the record. I do not own Rolaids. Or Paprika. And rarely use salt.

My Bar Mitzvah

"Today, I am a man," I said in a vocal range that ran from high alto to low baritone, all within the same sentence. I had a little peach fuzz above my upper lip, and my puberty hormones left me with a perpetual boner.

When a Jewish boy reaches the age of 13, he is called to up to the Pulpit to read from the Torah at a morning service. The Torah is the Old Testament, the five books of Moses, handwritten and rolled in a scroll as it has been for thousands of years. It always surprises me that so many of my Christian friends don't know that the Torah is simply the Old Testament. It is just written in Hebrew.

Modern Hebrew is hard enough to read, but at least it has vowels, notations under the squiggly letters to let you know which sounds to add - aye, ee, oo, ah, etc.

But that is not so in the Torah. This is old school Jewish. No vowels. It is a lot of guessing to get it right. I started Hebrew school at 9. At 13, I still could barely read it. Worse still, you don't read from the Torah. You chant from it. There are slight notations above the words to direct you how chant it or sing it. An ancient form of written music. Perhaps the earliest.

The portion of the Torah that I was to read on my special day was about ten minutes in length. Sheer terror. Plus, some prayers before and after the reading, all topped off by a speech I had to write and deliver telling everyone there how I was now a man.

I was a profoundly shy youngster. When I saw someone coming down the street towards me, I'd cross over to the other side so I wouldn't have to say hello. Think about a shy boy of 13 whose voice is changing. Now picture that boy chanting in a language he doesn't know in front of everyone in his life.

Yeah. I was in trouble!

Printed invitations to my Bar Mitzvah went out to about 100 family and friends.

> *Come watch me make an ass of myself. And then afterwards join us for a party to celebrate what was likely going to be my personal disaster.*

And then I discovered the Bar Mitzvah record. My saving grace. If you are not of my generation, a record is a big, black CD played on a record player or turntable. There was a recording for each Torah portion. I just had to give the guy my scheduled Bar Mitzvah date. Ten bucks later, I was in business.

I moved my brother's record player into my room and listened to the recording over and over again, dozens of times each day until I had it memorized.

My parents bought me my first suit: My Bar Mitzvah suit off the rack at Alexander's at the Green Acres Shopping Center. It didn't fit very well. It was one size too big. I suppose my parents thought I might get a wedding or a couple of funerals out of it before I outgrew it. But with a bright red tie and a crisp white shirt, it was the best I ever looked. If I was going to crash and burn, I would be dressed well for it.

Then the fateful day came. The 3rd Saturday in May. The morning service was scheduled to start promptly at 10 am. That would be 10 am JPT. Jewish People's Time, about 20 minutes later. How us Jews ever beat the Egyptians escaping to the other side of the Red Sea before Moses raised his staff and drowned them is a miracle unto itself. We are not a punctual people.

There I sat at the Bimah, the platform on which the Pulpit rests, staring out at the most important people in my life. Just as the service started, my mother's 300 lb. cousin Jeff, who occupied a large portion of the front row all by himself, shouted:

"Give the kid a fountain pen!"

A fountain pen was the traditional gift given to a Bar Mitzvah boy a few generations earlier. His wisecrack drew a little laughter, mostly from the old farts there. He was a funny guy. He was also the wealthiest in the family.

Jeff and June lived in a large house in Riverdale…. the most affluent section of The Bronx. They also had a summer place upstate we visited many times. I liked him. I once stole a Playboy magazine from him and he didn't rat me out.

Jeff gave me a $100 bill to celebrate the occasion. That was a crazy amount of money to give a 13-year-old boy, especially in 1964. June gave me a baseball signed by the 1943 Pittsburgh Pirates. She was a bit wild in her younger years. She 'dated' half the team. I still have the ball.

But I digress.

Our Synagogue was named Temple Torah, a storefront on Linden Boulevard converted from a closed hardware store. Nothing fancy. Everything there was second hand. From its first day, it remained a work in progress. Hanging electrical wires. Temporary walls. Folding chairs. But we all made the best of it.

The service got underway. All I had to do was sit there until my part came. About halfway through the 2-hour service, I glanced at my older brother, my dad, my grandfather, and Zayda, my great grandfather, all looking proud that I made it to this day. For hundreds of generations, we Jewish men (later women, too) stood before our congregations and chanted from the same scripture. I would now have a special bond with all of them. I too was beaming with pride.

It was my time to perform. I stepped up to the unfurled Torah scroll at the Pulpit. The Rabbi pointed to where I was to start. It didn't matter since I memorized it. And then it happened.

God looked down upon me and thought this would be a great time for my voice to crack. I sounded like a cartoon character. I spotted fat Jeff smiling, on the verge of laughter. The facial expressions of my family turned from pride to worry.

The Rabbi put his hand on my shoulder, which helped to ground me. I hunkered down and got through the rest of it with my high notes screeching like an owl in heat and my low tones sounding like a large bovine gasping for its last breath.

And then, just like that, it was over.

I don't remember much about the party back at our house. I had a few friends over. We ate too much deli and cake. But there wasn't much to do. So, we took the $100 bill I got from Jeff to Adaline's Candy Store a few blocks away on Linden Blvd. I wanted to treat my friends to some bubble gum. A bit obnoxious to be sure, but it was my special day.

Adaline took one look at us in suits with a $100 bill in hand and chased us out of her store with a string of curse words. I only knew half of them.

My friend's parents had checked in with my mom to see what I wanted as a Bar Mitzvah gift. She told them a basketball since mine could no longer stay inflated. I got three basketballs that day, along with some books (Jews love books), and some bonds that I would later cash in to buy beer when I was in college. I was told to save them for college. I did.

My grandmother gave me a couple of shares of AT&T.... Ma Bell. Four times a year, I got a 25-cent dividend check, about the value of a pack of baseball cards. But it was kind of cool. I owned a very small piece of one of the largest companies in the world.

My friends left in the afternoon. That's when the adults began to party. As they drank, it became more entertaining for me. A family friend, George Friedman, had *'mad professor hair'*. He looked like a cross between Larry of The Three Stooges and Albert Einstein.

He hadn't said a word to me in five years since I beat him at chess when I was eight.

He was perched on a bar stool next to our neighbor Penny. She had a very low-cut dress. He couldn't take his eyes off her boobs. I thought he was going to fall off the bar stool into her chest. My parents never entertained. It was nice to see them party with their friends. They cranked up the music on their hi-fi, ate, drank, and danced into the night. Our small house was full of laughter, joy, and celebration.

Harry, who cleaned our home on Fridays throughout my childhood, drank his weight in my dad's good Scotch, this time with my dad's permission. It was a celebration. He was dancing with no one in particular. Never saw a man so happy.

He told everyone that he was so proud.

"Harry would be so proud" is an expression that my family has used ever since whenever something wonderful happens to any of us.

All in all, it was a pretty good day!

The Flash

The first time I was on stage had been in Mrs. Simonetti's, 4th grade class. It was a silly play. Something about time and places around the world. I don't imagine there was a plot. Just kids dressed up taking a moment or two on stage.

Dressed like a person from China, I donned my Uncle Morris' silk, smoking jacket. It had an Asian design on it. My mother attached the Ponytail from one of my sister's dolls to the back of a black Yarmulke. With an eyebrow pencil, she drew a *fu man chu* mustache. Voila! I was Chinese, though I probably looked like a cross between Bonanza's Hop Sing and a confused Talmud student. Political correctness did not exist in the 1950s.

On cue, I was instructed to shuffle across the stage and mumble some words in Chinese. I had no idea what Chinese sounded like. There were no Asian kids in my school, so I never heard the language spoken.

What sounded like Chinese to my 10-year-old ears were the words "Va Fangool, Va Fangool." So, with the auditorium filled with parents, students, and teachers I loudly and proudly shouted the words "Va Fangool," over and over and over again as I shuffled across the stage. "Va Fangool" basically is Italian for *'go fuck yourself.'* It sounded Chinese to me.

At first, the adults in the audience were not sure if they heard me correctly. But by the third "Va Fangool" they roared with laughter.

Mrs. Simonetti could not get me off the stage fast enough. My mother was humiliated sitting in the audience among the ladies of the PTA. Naturally, I remained oblivious.

Thirty years later, I was on stage again. The Simsbury Theatre Guild gave me a role with one line in the Cole Porter musical *Anything Goes*. I got the role mostly because I showed up on time. I could sing baritone. And I had a penis. Women vastly outnumber men in community theater. They were happy to have me. All went well and I had fun.

The director called me some months later. She asked if I would be in a musical she was staging called *Is There Life After High School* at a theater in a neighboring town. The show uses songs and monologues to recall the joys, terrors, envies, hates, and loves that most teenagers experience throughout their four years of high school. The cast was comprised of five men and five women.

One of the highlights of the first act was a song the five men in the ensemble sing about their love of beer. It was choreographed with us singing, dancing, and palling around remembering our days drinking beer. As the song ended, one of the guys was to sneak up behind me and *"pants"* me…. pulling my sweatpants down exposing my Fred Flintstone boxer shorts. All went perfectly well in rehearsal. What could go wrong?

Whether it is Broadway, Off-Broadway, or in my case off-Hartford, actors get the jitters on opening night. It is scary to be on stage with an audience of several hundred.

We were doing great as the first act got underway. Then came the big number for the men, *"Beer."* I noticed a little extra energy with everyone. We were really into it, singing and dancing around at our fullest. As planned, one of my buddies came up behind me and yanked down my sweatpants. In his enthusiasm, he pulled down my underwear as well.

There I was, flashing my junk to an audience of 400. It is amazing how a moment of a second or two can feel like an hour or two. But there I was, naked from the waist down. And the audience went wild with laughter. I'm told someone actually fell off his chair guffawing.

That was the end of our song. The stage lights cut out as we hurriedly exited. I had three minutes to change and re-enter for my solo as two of the women took center stage with their monologues. As I stepped out on stage, spontaneous applause erupted. The audience clearly knew that my flashing them was a 'live theater' screw up. And they appreciated me going on with the show.

There was a part of me that wanted to run, go home and put a blanket over my head for a month. But I stayed with it and I sang my heart out. It was my first time singing a solo, a sweet song about the friends you meet in high school. I'm pretty sure that the applause I got had more to do with having the guts to get back on stage rather than the quality of my modest vocals.

In the years that followed, I found myself on stage in a dozen or more productions, including the role of a lifetime playing Tevye in *Fiddler on the Roof.* There are times when things on stage or off don't go as planned. It is at those moments when I shrug my shoulders and remember with fondness the wise words of my younger self.

And I say "Va Fangool."

Southern Comfort

Andy (16) and I (14) home alone for New Year's Eve weekend. One guess what we did. Yup. It was a hell of a party. My parents brought in 1966 taking our younger siblings Tom and Amy to the Poconos. A little winter getaway for them; an opportunity to go a little crazy for us.

We started planning the party a few days in advance. We dared not get into my father's bar. He had been keeping a sharper eye on his bottles lately. Our cleaning man, Harry, would periodically pour himself into oblivion on my father's best hooch. The drinking age in New York was 18. Rarely enforced. Andy's plan was to order liquor over the phone and have it delivered. Our invitees put in their orders and paid in advance.

The order read something like: a six pack of Rheingold, pint of Seagram's 7, their cheapest Vodka and Rum, nips of Schnapps, bottles of Mateus Rosé and Blue Nun, and a small bottle of Southern Comfort. That was for me. I don't know why, but it sounded cool. Oh, and a pack of Marlboro in a box. That was more or less the order.

Imagine my 16-year-old brother calling that in, faking he was my dad. Nothing suspicious there. He said, "Me and the Mrs. are having some friends over for New Year's Eve." The scheduled delivery was for 8:00 PM. Sharp. That very evening.

Our friends arrived. We told some jokes, horsed around, and played nickel ante poker. About a quarter of 8:00, we quieted everyone down. The delivery was expected shortly. Like clockwork, the doorbell rang at 8:00 pm. Sharp. Andy turned on the bathroom shower full blast with the door wide open. I was the youngest and most innocent looking I suppose so I answered the front door.

"Hey dad, your delivery is here," I shouted up the staircase in too loud a voice. I had not yet honed my acting skills.

"I'm in the shower. Pay him. My wallet is on the kitchen table," he said in his best Dad voice.

I handed the delivery guy our money, a large pile of fives and ones that had been carefully counted out in advance. Plus, a nice tip. I don't think we fooled him. He couldn't have been much more than 18 anyway. And certainly, he couldn't have cared less about a bunch of kids getting shit-faced on New Year's Eve.

And the party went on. We drank, played some more poker, smoked cigarettes, and ate junk food late into the night. One by one we found places around the house to pass out. Except Ira. He hugged the porcelain throne. And slept the night away on the bathroom floor.

Other than sipping Manischewitz at Passover, this was my first-time drinking. I got through most of the bottle of Southern Comfort. It kicked my ass. I felt like Sonny Liston after seven rounds with Muhammad Ali. Everyone started moving around by mid-morning. Slowly. And we cleared them out. Andy and I had to get the house cleaned. Our parents would be home in roughly five hours.

We tore through the house with sponges, mop, and vacuum, demonstrating an awesome display of brotherly teamwork. A few hours later, the house was cleaner and tidier than my parents had left it two days earlier. **Mistake #1.**

We opened all the windows to air out the stale smell of cigarettes, booze, and the lingering scent of Ira's vomit. New Year's in New York is not a great time to open all the windows. **Mistake #2.** As the cold air poured in, our heating system cranked itself up to high. Blasting out heat. A couple of hours later, we closed all the windows in the house, just as my parents pulled into the driveway.

My mother came in first and got blasted by the heat from our furnace. A quick peek around the now spotless house and she demanded to know what went on here over the weekend. My head was pounding. Whatever I ate for breakfast was churning angrily in my stomach, but I still came up with a somewhat believable answer.

"We wanted to surprise you for the New Year. Andy and I cleaned the whole house. Happy New Year, Mom."

I got that one out with a straight face. Lying to your mother. Is that one of the Ten Commandments? I never could keep those straight. Did they really mean not to covet your neighbor's ass? Cause Cathy next door was hot. So confusing for a teenage boy. Anyway. I thought we were in the clear. Until my dad walked in. Dad was a twenty-year veteran of the NYPD who didn't miss a thing.

"How was the party, boys?" he said as he looked around, impressed at how well we cleaned up after ourselves.

On the way into the house, he peeked in the trash can which was loaded with empty liquor bottles. We were busted.

I was not going to make **Mistake #3** and try to tell him that our neighbors must have used our trash can. We were grounded for two weeks and couldn't have friends over for a month. It was a hell of a party. But to this day my stomach still does flips at the mere sight of a bottle of Southern Comfort.

The Hooks Are in The Back, Stupid

I was still just a boy. A couple of years past my bar mitzvah with a girl on a fast track into womanhood. Here's the back story.

In my sophomore year in high school, I joined a fraternity where my brother Andy was a brother. This was a great bunch of guys and we did some extraordinary things. Sigma Alpha Rho was a Jewish fraternity founded by Philadelphia high school boys early in the 20th century. Anti-Semitism kept them out of other fraternities, so they started their own.

SAR had chapters throughout the U.S. and Canada. We would take bus trips to visit chapters in other cities for weekend get togethers called conclaves. We would stay in their homes and be set up with dates from local sororities to the parties they'd throw. Of course, we'd reciprocate periodically, filling our parent's homes with scores of our out-of-town fraternity brothers.

The highlight of these weekend conclaves would be large dances we would put together. We would rent a hall, hire a band, and sell hundreds of tickets. The only parental involvement in this process was a contractual obligation for chaperones.

We once booked The Chiffon's, a major Motown act with numerous hit records. Remember *"Sweet Talking Guy?"* More than a thousand high school kids from all over Queens attended, jackets and ties required. There tended to be fewer fights when we were dressed up. The money we raised that night went toward purchasing an ambulance for our community.

Once a year, the fraternity would have a national convention. I was the youngest of twenty who attended from our chapter in Queens that year. I took my first plane ride, a four-engine prop from JFK on a one-hour flight to Washington DC.

Here's what happened.

The convention was held at the Washington Hilton Hotel where some years later John Hinkley attempted to assassinate Ronald Reagan. Over 500 fraternity brothers arrived from all over the country and Canada. The rules were pretty, simple: No alcohol. No girls in the rooms. Act like gentlemen. Yada. Yada. Yada. All I heard was, "Don't get caught."

Each of the brothers was set up with a date for the big Saturday night dance with a sorority girl from a local high school.

My date Cheryl was from Chevy Chase – sounds like the beginning of a tongue twister. It's an up-scale suburb and a $10 cab ride from DC. I asked the cab driver to wait as I knocked on the door to a house that dwarfed my home in Queens. I was met by her pipe smoking father in the large, tiled foyer under a gaudy glass chandelier, the kind I had seen at Leonard's of Great Neck, an over-the-top banquet facility famous for its opulent weddings. He slipped me a $20 bill for cab fare and called to his daughter.

She was a very well-developed sixteen-year-old. She looked twenty, bursting out of her low cut, full-length evening gown. In the cab ride back to DC I soon discovered that I was way out of my league. I was a boy just a bit past my bar mitzvah. While she was on a fast track to womanhood.

Within a half hour of our arrival back at the Hilton, we snuck past security and took the elevator up to my room. A part of me was hoping that we would get stopped and sent back to the dance. The other part of me was a horny teenager anxious to see what would happen next.

She had consumed two nips of scotch stolen from her father's collection. She called them his "airplane bottles." We kissed for a very long time before I took a shot and courageously touched her breast. She abruptly stood up. I fully expected to get kicked. Instead, she removed her dress. She was wearing her older sister's prom dress and didn't want to ruin it.

For the next half hour, I tried every way possible to remove her bra. But never having seen one, I couldn't imagine how it worked. Cheryl was giving me no clues. I think she was enjoying my predicament. Finally, my roommate barged in. I was in college before I learned that you hang a tie on the doorknob if you had a girl in the room.

Cheryl was dressed and gone in a flash. By the time she hit the elevator doors, my roommate had already told everyone he could find. That I had gotten laid.

The older guys wanted to know how I got a girl into my room. And if I really had sex. I blushed, unable to be honest about how little I really knew about girls. Saying nothing led my fellow fraternity brothers to draw their own conclusions. I was a woman killer. Babe hound. Lady's man. All the typical expressions of the day.

None of them accurate.

When I got home, I found one of my mother's bras in the laundry hamper. The hooks were in the back. Who knew? That information would not become useful for several more years. Figuring out women would be a lifelong adventure.

Sigma Alpha Rho Fraternity
Upsilon Kappa Chapter
PRESENTS
EMPIRE BALL
STARRING
THE CHIFFONS
THE DEL SATINS

MUSIC BY - SCOTCH 'N THE ROCKS

SATURDAY, MARCH 12, 1966

THE   CORDONBLEU
JAMACIA AVE & 96TH STREET

8;00 P.M.   DONATION $2.50

N⁰. 0288

Swimming Naked

Had this happened today, it would have been a front-page story. A scandal. Maybe even an arrest or two. It was my high school gym class where one day a week the boys all swam together. Naked. The last thing a 14-year-old freshman wants to do is hop naked in a cold pool with 100 other boys. But that was a requirement at Andrew Jackson High School in the 1960s.

The pool was small. Twenty-five yards long and four swimming lanes wide. The diving area encompassed a third of the pool. It was over our heads, forcing us to cluster in the shallow (4') end, frolicking naked together.

Mr. Smith was our gym teacher. It was rumored that he took a bronze medal for swimming in the 1948 Olympics. He didn't. I looked it up. He was a creepy guy. He would walk the perimeter of the pool, smacking each boy in the ass with a Styrofoam paddle to keep them in the pool. More than once, I pulled a classmate who couldn't swim to the side of the pool. Nothing heroic. I just reached out to flailing arms and panicked eyes.

Most young teenagers have body issues. I was no different. I admit to being uncomfortable walking around and swimming in the nude. The cold pool water didn't help, either. Yes, there was considerable shrinkage. And yes, anyone who didn't sneak a peek was a liar. There were a few older boys. Seniors. More like full grown men. They strode in together with their enormous uncircumcised swinging *schlongs*. You could hear an occasional *"Holy Shit"* above the din of the splashing. These guys were big and heavily muscled. But they couldn't swim very well.

One day, the coach had us line up four abreast. At the sound of his whistle, we took off and raced the length of the pool. I learned to swim as a child in summer camp and was a pretty good swimmer. With a good racing dive and a dozen or so strong freestyle strokes, I beat the three others in my heat by more than a body length. I had the fastest time of anyone there that day, and I was invited to join the swim team.

There were benefits to being on the swim team. I no longer had to be in that stupid gym class in a pile of naked boys. I could wear a green speedo bathing suit, and I would wear a sateen green Andrew Jackson High School letter jacket.

The team needed a second breast stroker to compete. Figuring I'd have a lifetime of telling people I stroked breasts in high school, I volunteered. Besides, the guys who swam freestyle were much faster. And I also bumped my head doing flip turns.

Each afternoon we'd practice, lap after lap. I swam the 100-yard breaststroke. Four lengths in the overly chlorinated pool water. No goggles. No swim cap. I swam about a mile a day…. roughly 70 laps. But I was slow.

Someone suggested that I shave my legs to shave some time off the clock. I did. It didn't. It took a year for the hair to grow back.

Swimming was a winter sport. It was dark by the time practice ended, and in 1968 there were no hair dryers. By the time I walked two blocks from the high school to catch the bus on Linden Blvd, my hair would be frozen solid. It wasn't cool to wear a hat. I was also allergic to the chlorine in the pool. After each swim, my eyes were thoroughly blood shot. Each streetlight and headlight had a fuzzy halo around it.

Our swim meets were predictable. I finished in fourth place (dead last) in the breaststroke each time we competed. That is until the last meet of the season. It was against Bayside High School, one of the best swim teams in the city. If there was smart money to bet that afternoon, it would not have been bet on me.

Halfway through the meet was the 100-yard breaststroke. The four of us took our marks. We got set, and before the starter pistol was shot, one of the Bayside guys jumped in early and was disqualified. This race was to be my 'swan song'. My last time competing. I would not finish fourth.

My team cheered me as I touched the wall two body lengths behind the second-place finisher. A respectable third place. I chose to see it as a bronze medal finish, rather than another last place. When the team points were totaled, Bayside High School beat us by a hefty margin. But on that day, I took a third place, and I wore my Andrew Jackson High School letter jacket with pride.

I recently came across my old letter jacket which had been buried in the back of my closet for decades. Of course, it no longer fits. Not even close. But trying it on reminded me of the day of my great victory.

The day I did not finish last.

The Andrew Jackson High School swim team. I'm top row third from the left

Bad Decisions and Reckless Moments

By the grace of God. I survived.

I made it through a lifetime of reckless moments and bad decisions without spending a night in the hospital or a day in jail. Here is a sampling. The statutes of limitations have long since expired.

In the first grade, we used to play tag. The color red was a safe base. Hanging on to anything red kept you in the game. We were very competitive. Once my neighbor's red Ford Falcon moved from its usual parking spot, the closest red item I could hold on to was the fire alarm box on the corner. When two of us tried to grab onto it, somehow it got pulled. Ten minutes later, fire engines raced down our street. Pissed off firemen walked our street looking for the culprits. We hid in my basement for hours.

In the 4th grade, I killed Red Sox Slugger, Carl Yastrzemski. I should explain that one. Jones Beach had an archery range in those days. On the way back to the car, I picked up an errant arrow which landed near our parking space. Once home, I built a crossbow, crossed sticks and rubber bands looped together. The girls in the playground used to call it a Chinese jump rope. Mine was double thick. When attached to my crossbow, it created a fairly powerful weapon.

I placed my Carl Yastrzemski baseball card (never cared for the Red Sox) in front of a thin pillow on the far side of my small bedroom. I then loaded my arrow and drew it back with all my might. When I let go, it shot through Carl Yastrzemski's head, the pillow, and buried itself deep into my bedroom wall. I created a pea-sized hole in my house which I later filled with half a tube of McLean's Whitening toothpaste I found in my parent's bathroom. That did the trick, and the minty scent freshened up the stale air in my otherwise smelly bedroom.

I carried a switchblade in Junior High. Not so much for protection, but to be cooler than I actually was. It was my little secret. At least for a while. I guess I could blame my mother. She brought home a plastic silverware holder too large for the kitchen drawer. Naturally, I volunteered to cut it down to size. The blade ended up an inch deep in my left thigh. Three stiches later, I had a scar and limped for a month. But I got to tell my friends I got stabbed with a switchblade. My parents grounded me. And took away my knife.

This stupidity continued into high school but got a bit more serious. Hanging out with a couple of friends one day, the conversation turned to cars. My buddy Mike bragged that his cousin taught him how to hot wire a car. Tony and I didn't believe it. One dare led to another. Next thing we knew, we three idiots were driving in someone else's car. Without permission. Without a key. And without licenses. The car stalled a couple of blocks away. We jumped out and ran and hoped the police would not dust for prints like they did on the TV show, "Dragnet." I never hung out with those two dopes again.

I smoked a lot of pot as a freshman in college. Buying an ounce at a time got expensive and money was tight. Rather than cut back on usage, I came up with a foolproof plan, only to discover that I was the fool in foolproof.

A friend and I chipped in and bought a pound of pot. We figured that we could bag it into 16-ounce units, make some money, and smoke for free. So, we purchased a pound, thankfully, not from an undercover cop. As we emptied the contents of the one-pound bag on the kitchen table to divide it, we discovered several three-ounce nails mixed in. There was no profit. In the history of pot peddlers in 1969, we might have been the only idiots to actually lose money.

There were a couple of shoplifting moments. And the time I started a fire in my house playing with matches. And I guess I'd have to add in the destruction of public property. I hurled a rock through the window of my second-grade classroom at P.S. 176 after my teacher smacked me with a ruler for spelling SHIRT on the blackboard without the R.

I consider myself extraordinarily lucky not to have gotten seriously hurt or in serious trouble through my bad decisions. And my reckless moments. I never considered myself a "bad ass," but if a few of the above moments went sideways, the above could have been a police rap sheet rather than the abundance of juvenile stupidity I survived.

The Tuba

I was not a very attentive student, and I had the grades to prove it. High School for me was largely a social activity. I could hang with my friends. When we got bored, we'd leave to Jones Beach or into the city. Or to a pool room a few blocks away.

Andrew Jackson High School was a large urban school of 4,000 students in a three-story building in St. Albans, Queens. It was crowded, noisy, and chaotic and an easy place to hide under the radar screen. I would change the grades on my report card and I got pretty good at forging my mother's scribbled signature. It was easy street.

Then reality hit me like a punch in the face.

These were the Vietnam War years with half a million young Americans taking up arms half a world away. At age 18, young men were required to sign up for the Selective Service. The Draft!

However, if you were enrolled in college, you were classified with a 2-S standing, which meant you couldn't be drafted. If you didn't, you received a 1-A designation. 1-A meant you were available to be given a uniform and a gun. After six weeks of basic training, you'd be thrown into the meat grinder called "Nam" where over 50,000 Americans would eventually be killed. This I wanted no part of.

I had to find a way into college. Though I was on both the baseball and swim teams, I was nowhere good enough to be considered for a college scholarship. My grades clearly were not impressive either. I needed an edge, something that would set me apart and get me into college to acquire the coveted 2-S designation. It was rapidly becoming a life and death issue.

The first day of my Junior year, I was assigned to a shop class located in the basement of the high school - next to the music room. Since I was pretty sure I'd lose a body part in the shop class, I asked Mrs. Gluck, the band director, if I could transfer and take a music class rather than shop.

She encouraged me to try the Tuba. I had a good ear for music having taught myself how to play the guitar some years earlier. So, I gave it a shot. Within a month, I was the band's tuba player. It came easily to me. I also thought that if I did get drafted, I might play Tuba in the Army Band. No one shoots tuba players.

In the summer between my Junior and Senior year in high school, I took a job as a dishwasher in a Music camp in Maine. In return for my kitchen labor, I could take classes and music lessons.

The classes in theory, harmony, and orchestration with really talented musicians were challenging and fun. But what I benefited most from was a summer of private lessons on an old, dented Tuba I borrowed from my high school and schlepped up to Maine on a Greyhound bus.

I spent the entire summer working on a complicated audition piece. One note at a time I practiced an hour a day, every day for eight weeks. By the end of the summer, I dramatically improved as a Tuba player and my audition piece was damn near perfect. After eight weeks of toiling, it was time to make the music or face the music.

In September of my Senior year, I auditioned for the All-City High School Band. To my complete surprise, I was accepted. I got to play with the best high school musicians in New York City. I think this annoyed my girlfriend, Liz. She was a talented and serious violinist who was accepted to the All-City Orchestra. I had only been playing the tuba for just a year.

Soon after I applied for admission to the University of Hartford in hopes of one day transferring to its world-renowned, Hartt School of Music. I was accepted. A month later, I received my 2-S designation from the Selective Service. For the next four years, I would be safe from the draft. So long as I stayed in school, I would not become embroiled in the horror that was the Vietnam War.

Playing the Tuba was a means to an end. It got me to where I needed to be. And life went on. I did not play another note on the Tuba for forty years until I joined the Simsbury Community Band.

All these years later, I still think about that over-confident 16-year-old. On some level, I must have known that playing a 30 lb. twist of brass tubes would change the trajectory of my life. And it did. Today when I play my Tuba, the large silver mouthpiece screens my joyful smile.

With the Simsbury Community Band

On The Job

Everyone I grew up with had an after school or weekend job. As youngsters, we baby sat, mowed, shoveled, delivered papers. Whatever gave us walking around money. By 16, I could get a 'real job.' In the years that followed, I was hired and fired too many times to mention. Here is an entertaining sampling:

I worked as a stock boy on Saturdays at Best & Company, a department store (since demolished) a few blocks from Rockefeller Center. I would eat an early lunch in the subsidized cafeteria and then take my afternoon break in the employee lounge where I'd fall fast asleep until 4pm in a comfy chair just in time to punch out. No one ever missed me.

I was hired on an assembly line of a company that put wedding albums together. My job was in the lacquer booth. Photos were placed upright on a conveyor belt. As they passed by, I would apply a thin coat of lacquer. This was pre-OSHA. Limited workplace rules and not much ventilation. After spraying a couple of wedding albums, I was pretty stoned from the fumes.

All these families pretty much looked the same. I assigned names to the typical characters that would appear at almost every wedding. There was drunk Uncle Harry. Overly made-up Aunt Rose. Penny with her boobs falling out of her dress. And, of course, the hot bridesmaid and the horny best man trying to bang her.

In my mind, I would sing *Hava Negela* and songs from *Fiddler on the Roof*, entertaining myself as the photos rolled by on the conveyor belt. Happy families dancing together in joyous celebration.

By the third or fourth wedding, I was really high. The songs would be out loud in full voice. Eventually, they fired me which probably saved my life. I killed off far too many brain cells.

I lied about my age and worked stacking cases of beer in the warehouse of a wholesale beer distributor. I told them I was 18. The first day on the job, a stack of cases got bumped by a forklift. The top case fell off. From a height of about 10 feet, I got hit in the head with a six-pack as the case fell apart mid-air. I worked the rest of the day. When I got home and mentioned the incident at dinner, I was whisked away to the hospital. They shaved a hole in my haircut and treated me to half a dozen sutures on the top of my head. My dad made me quit that job. I was underage, anyway.

Someday, I will lose my hair and an ugly scar will appear, a reminder of the day a six pack of Rheingold landed on my thick head.

The father of a friend made his living putting on dances and small concerts at the Riverside Hotel ballroom in Spanish Harlem. He needed four or five young guys to set up and serve.

These Saturday night jobs went from 7 pm until about 3 am. He picked us up and drove us in his enormous Cadillac. Biggest car I ever sat in. I was the youngest and therefore relegated to manning the coat room.

After taking in 300 to 400 coats, I had time on my hands before the rush at the end of the night. I got to hear some of the best Black, Puerto Rican, and Reggae musicians of the day wailing on their instruments to the wee hours of the New York morning. My all-time favorite was Tito Puente.

After coats were distributed, tips collected, and the ballroom returned to its original condition, we left. Julie, the boss, parked his Cadillac right at the front door. This was not a safe neighborhood and Julie carried the evening's proceeds in cash. A lot of cash. But nobody messed with him. So, we white boys from Queens stuck close to his side.

On the way home, we'd stop at an all-night diner near Kennedy Airport. At that hour, they served mostly cops, cabbies, and hookers. We swapped jokes, laughing ourselves into giddy exhaustion, arriving back home to see the sun rise over the Belt Parkway. And I'd sleep until noon.

But my favorite high school job was my last. The summer before attending college, I was a waiter at Klar Crest Resort in Moodus, CT. The little town of Moodus had a half dozen family resorts. It was a poor man's 'borscht belt'. More affluent families headed to the Catskills.

Families would come up for a week by car or bus from the city. It was an all-inclusive experience. It looked and felt like the resort featured in the movie *Dirty Dancing*. I had three tables of 10 to serve three meals a day. At week's end, I'd look for my small brown envelope, a tip from each couple. Usually, $15 or $20.

I was a lousy waiter. Forgetful. A bit clumsy. But I charmed the men and flirted harmlessly with their wives. I banked enough to get me through my first year at the University of Hartford. Sunday night was lobster night. I had never had a lobster before. There was a woman at one of my tables. Her husband had gone back early to the city. She stayed on for a few more days. I chatted with her a bit, clearly remembering seeing her poolside in her bikini earlier in the day.

She said she didn't like lobster and that I should bring her a steak instead. When I shared with her that I had never had lobster, she said to bring her one "to go." I could pick it up at her cabin after the meal hour. I eagerly agreed and didn't give it another thought.

I showed up later at her cabin. She was dressed in a very low-cut blouse. Tight shorts. She was 36. Twice my age. It was reminiscent of the movie *Mrs. Robinson*, which I recently seen. My first bite of lobster was delicious. But I immediately lost interest. She seduced me. My very own Mrs. Robinson affair.

I no longer remember her name. But I can never forget that date. It was July 20, 1969. At the very hour Apollo 11 gently touched down on the surface of the moon, I gently touched down on my own Mrs. Robinson. She was my first. And a billion people around the planet cheered for Neil Armstrong.

And for me.

1956 Plymouth

A Very Used Car

Maybe it's just a guy thing, but I remember more about my first car than my first girlfriend, though clearly, my first girlfriend was a lot prettier than my first car.

First, I should tell you that my first car was not a used car. It was a *'very used'* car. My brother Andy and I pooled our cash and agreed to share the expenses.

We were into it for a total of $35.00 Yes, $17.50 each bought us our first car. To say that it was beat to crap would give crap some intrinsic value. It was a two-tone (red and white) 1956 Plymouth with push button gears. The odometer on the 12-year-old car stopped recording at 60,000 miles, though it more than likely had two or three times that much in hard earned NYC mileage.

There was a small hole in the muffler which noisily announced my arrival from half a block away. When stopped at a red light next to a souped-up muscle car, I would rev the engine proclaiming that I was ready to drag race the moment the light turned green.

Frequently, a guy next to me would tear out, leaving a 10' patch of rubber. I'd putter ahead at a glacial speed. My car could go from 0-50 mph in about the time it would take to eat a sandwich. I once got pulled over by NY's finest along with a drag racer I had just coaxed into a race. He got a speeding ticket. I was told to fix my muffler.

The car had no seatbelts and the brakes needed to be pumped several times in order to engage. This car was truly unsafe at any speed.

On many a summer day, I would park in the driveway where I'd be in direct sun. I'd lay on the hood of my car with aluminum folding reflectors under my chin. It was the original tanning bed.

The car had no power steering which made parallel parking on the crowded streets of Queens extra challenging. I would generally look for a space I could pull into. Andy, on the other hand, enjoyed parallel parking. He would pull in backwards until he hit the car behind him. Then straighten out pulling forward until he bumped the car in front. These bumps on each car fender would push the cars further and further away, thereby enlarging the parking space. It was quite entertaining to watch, unless you owned a car on either side my brother's driving.

Andy would dance as he drove, guiding the car from side to side to the beat of the latest Motown hits on our staticky AM radio. He once knocked down a highway lamppost on the Cross-Island Parkway. The front end of our car was pushed in just enough for the fan to click against the radiator while it spun around. Once home, we wrapped a heavy chain around a large tree to the underside of the car. He slowly backed up. The chain held. The tree held and the car gradually straightened out. The loud noise brought out neighbors who enjoyed the show we put on. A few minutes later, the old car was good to go.

On a quiet night, my friends and I loved to just drive around. We'd often drive from Shell station to Shell station collecting special aluminum presidential coins. Shell's *"Mr. President"* coin game. They gave one coin to each paying customer. We'd put a quarter of gas in the tank each time we stopped, hoping for a shot to win the $1,000 James Madison instant winner. That never happened, though we once got a Chester A. Arthur which instantly netted us $1.00.

At a red light or stop sign, someone would invariably yell, "Chinese Fire Drill." All four doors would fly open, and we'd run around the car twice before jumping back in and driving off. Food was a large part of mindlessly driving around. Our two favorite stops were Jahn's Old Fashioned Ice Cream Parlor on Queens Blvd. in Forrest Hills and Nathan's on Long Beach Rd. in Oceanside.

Jahn's was famous for their enormous special '*The Kitchen Sink*.' It was presented in a huge silver bowl large enough to hold a basketball, filled to the brim with scoops of various ice cream flavors, toppings and syrups crowned with a six-inch layer of whipped cream and sprinkles. Typically, it would take five of us to make a dent in one.

If you were heroic enough to successfully consume an entire '*Kitchen Sink*' by yourself, you'd get a second one. Free of charge. Rarely did that happen. I was never man enough to try. Nathan's of Oceanside was an institution filled with young people nightly from the far corners of Queens and Long Island. Oceanside was one of the 'Five Towns,' ritzy-titsy communities where the *nouveau-riche* from Queens and Brooklyn moved to get away from the likes of us.

Nathan's served their famous Hot Dogs along with other deli offerings and desserts. It was an early version of a food court under one expansive roof. We generally arrived in a caravan of cars, quickly claiming a few of the picnic tables where we would consume copious amounts of food.

It was a great place to try picking up girls. Major problem was we were not that swift. Our cars, especially mine, screamed of lower middle-class Queens. The kids from Long Island dressed better, had stylish haircuts, and drove fancier cars. I hated them.

Most evenings, we just hung out on 234th street in Laurelton in front of the homes of a couple of girls we were buddies with. One memorable night after being teased about how ugly my car was, we decided to paint it. Under the streetlights, we repainted my car with latex house paint. I also thought it would be a great idea to paint a giant peace sign on the trunk. After all, this was 1968. In small letters under the peace sign I wrote the words *'of ass.'* It seemed like a good idea at the time.

I drove home. Pulled up in front of my house. Now it could have been the illegal substance I had inhaled earlier that evening, or it could have been the glow of the streetlight shining on the still wet surface of my '56 Plymouth. But my car simply took my breath away. A work of art. It was beautiful. It was perfect.

And then it rained.

Streaks of white and red paint dripped, combining into a complete mess. The windows needed to be scraped with a razor blade in order for the car to be drivable. The only area that remained in good shape was the trunk. With a Peace sign. And the words 'of ass' under it.

I had never seen my brother so pissed off. He was a college man and relied on our vehicle as his means of transportation to Queens College that morning. I scraped the windows and he drove off to school. We never spoke of it again.

At the end of the school year, we sold the car to a junk yard. We received its scrap metal value.

$35.00

Today, I drive a luxury car with leather seats, a 6-speaker stereo system and brakes you only must depress once in order to stop. It cost more than the home I grew up in.

Perhaps after five or six owners, when my new car becomes a *'very used car'* it will end up as a teenager's first car. And a driving experience he'll cherish for a lifetime.

Freshman Class

My daily mantra, *"Don't fuck this up,"* rattled in my head.

The year was 1969. Young men not enrolled in college were "Draft bait" and likely headed to Vietnam. I had my 2-S draft designation. I was safe. That is, so long as I stayed in school.

"Don't fuck this up."

I hauled my duffel bag and guitar up four flights of stairs to my first home in Hartford, a rooming house used by the University of Hartford to house its overflow, 80 incoming freshmen, several miles from campus.

Like most colleges at the time, the University of Hartford was stretched beyond its capacity. There was no more room on campus, so we were housed in an old building on aptly named Asylum Avenue in Hartford. And an asylum it was.

The old rooming house, Stowe Hall was named for the author of *Uncle Tom's Cabin*. Harriet Beecher Stowe. She and Mark Twain had homes next to each other about a mile away.

I was happy. With a new sense of freedom, a fresh start with four years to learn what I could and then figure out where my life would take me.

Stowe Hall was a strange place with a slew of oddball characters. My first week there, I came across one of the resident advisors (dorm counselor). He was naked, wrapped in a sheet, vomiting on the bathroom floor as he tried to kick his addiction to heroin. We later nicknamed him "Cold Turkey." He was gone before mid-terms.

At precisely 4:00 pm, two of the inbound lanes on Asylum Avenue would reverse direction. The city fathers thought this would be the best way to move rush hour traffic out of Hartford. In the blink of an eye, all four lanes were headed westbound.

A couple of times a week, a confused motorist would try to maneuver against four lanes of traffic, looking like a blind salmon swimming upstream. One of the enterprising guys in our building sold Polaroid snap shots of the car accidents for insurance settlements. This earned him beer and pizza money.

A guy named Tony brought his motorcycle to school. Periodically, he would drive through the building. It was very noisy. Surprising. And very funny.

A few of us took a large oil portrait of the founding college President. It hung in my room for a few days. Once we realized that its monetary value could result in a charge of grand larceny, it was moved to our lounge.

We anonymously called in the crime. They sent a security officer to pick it up later, admitting that they hadn't known it was missing, so, there was no reward for its safe return. Though we tried. That very portrait now hangs high on a wall in the University Library, safe from fearless freshmen with too much time on their hands.

One night after too much beer drinking, one dare led to another. A guy named Paul said he'd run naked from our front door to the back door of Arthur's Drug Store two blocks away. For $80. Fifteen minutes later, the money was collected.

Dressed in nothing more than a Tri-cornered hat, a scarf, and a big smile, off he went with dozens of us cheering him on. Upon his return, there was a police car at the corner. Paul politely tipped his hat and scooted back into Stowe Hall. The cops took a moment to analyze the situation, broke out in laughter, and drove off, giving them a great story to bring home.

I'm not saying that Paul was the first streaker in America, but this was 1969. None of us ever heard of anything that crazy before. Some years later, streaking would become a rite of passage on campuses across the country. The fad petered out (no pun intended) by the mid-70's after someone streaked the Academy Awards on live TV.

Transportation to campus was our thumbs. Hitching to campus generally took a while, particularly in nasty weather or at odd hours. Our meals were generally taken at the luncheon counter at Arthur's Drug store, the variety/drug store Paul streaked to. It was a couple of blocks away.

Though we were all somewhat jealous of the thousands of other freshmen sleeping in warm dorms on campus and eating together in the cafeterias, living off campus was more of an adventure.

And then came the cold November winds, a prelude of the winter ahead. Stowe Hall was not heated very well. The single pane windows did little to hold in the warmth. There was no doubt that it was going to be very unpleasant in the months to come.

Ten weeks into our freshman year in college, a dozen of us decided to take some action. We were going to take over the Student Union on campus and demand better conditions.

The voice in my head, *"Don't fuck this up"* grew louder. I ignored it.

It was evening, so hitchhiking was out of the question. One of my buddies, Bob said that his girlfriend lived in nearby West Hartford. He was sure her mother would drive a bunch of us to campus. A few of the guys had cars, so they headed up as the rest of us waited for our ride.

I had read about leftwing, antiwar student takeovers at Columbia, Berkeley, and NYU. By contrast, we were a sorry lot. There we were, waiting with pillows and blankets in hand for someone's mother to drive us to our protest. It felt more like a sleepover than a revolution.

And then a VW minibus painted in psychedelic Day-Glo colors rounded the corner, slamming on its brakes in front of our building. Our mouths dropped. We had been expecting a proper West Hartford mom with pearls and a sweater set driving a Volvo station wagon. What we got was Jayne, a large woman in a Michigan football jacket smoking a cigarette. The side door slid open. With our pillows and blankets, we piled in.

She said something like:

"So, are you guys going to burn the fucking place down?"

In the years that followed, I got to know and love Jayne and her entire family. I shared many holiday meals with them. For the 30 years that followed - until the last one of them left the area - I was treated like a member of the family.

But on this night, I said, "No ma'am. We just want heat in our dorm building."

She dropped us off. We joined the rest of our group. It was 10:00 pm. The Student Union building was mostly empty. We set up our bedding not knowing what to expect.

I had images of police barging in with nightsticks flying. What we got was Chet, an old man in an ill-fitting security uniform. He came over and asked who was in charge. Since everyone took a step back, I guess that was me. We chatted a for a bit. He knew we were there to make our point, not to make a big mess.

He said:

"See that chair over there? I'm going to sleep in it. Don't do anything to fuck up this place or I could lose my job. And I need this job."

"Yes sir," was all I could muster. His request was quite reasonable.

Chet and I became buddies for the remainder of my days at the University.

The next morning, Chet woke us up and said the President of the

University would like to meet the group's leaders in his office at 9:00 am. I washed the sleep out of my eyes and gave my pillow to someone else to take back to Stowe Hall. It was agreed that I'd be our spokesperson. Three of us marched across the campus to meet with President Woodruff, a short man with a bushy, white mustache.

Who could have known that three years later he and I would square off with custard pies, resulting in a four-page spread in *Life Magazine*? But that is another story.

Our demands were simple. We wanted working heat and a commuter van to take us to and from school several times a day. He agreed. It was all too easy. I should have asked for a half million dollars, a plane to Cuba, and a pony for my sister. But I took the win. And life went on.

The next week I was elected to the Student Senate.

Some years later, Stowe Hall was torn down. The 'highest and best' use for that property was as a small parking lot. Each time I pass that parking lot on Asylum Avenue, I think about the crazy times I shared half a century ago with 80 freshmen who possessed an abundance of good humor. Fearlessness.

And class.

My freshman year at the University of Hartford

The Great Pie Duel

It began with Woodstock. Hippies. *'Love-Ins.'* Flower Power. Soon after escalating into antiwar demonstrations, riots, takeover of buildings, and the killing of fellow students at Kent State and Jackson State. It was a tumultuous time.

I hitchhiked with a buddy from Hartford to Washington DC to join 500,000 others in a loud and boisterous antiwar demonstration. We even tried to levitate the Pentagon. It didn't work. There was lots of pot. Girls without bras. Sharp shooters on rooftops. And some teargas.

These were my college years.

I joined Students for a Democratic Society (SDS) and sauntered around in a drab green Army jacket adorned with a black fist in the middle of my back. My hair grew longer. I became an angry young man. My new heroes were Che, Mao, Ho, and Fidel. Looking back, I was a bit of a caricature. A rebel without a clue. But that was what life was like in those days.

In between the sex, drugs, and rock 'n' roll, we somehow managed to get an education. It was a frenzied, chaotic and exhausting time.

In my senior year, I was elected President of the Student Government.

This was the year Richard Nixon ran for reelection. His challenger was an antiwar candidate, George McGovern. We loved McGovern and did what we could to get him elected.

It was Nixon's crew that got caught breaking into the Democratic National Committee's offices at The Watergate complex. The ensuing scandal would eventually lead to Nixon resigning in disgrace.

The first Tuesday in November, Richard Nixon trounced George McGovern, winning all but one state: Massachusetts. Our efforts to end the War and create a more inclusive society evaporated overnight.

The angst on campus was palpable. Tensions grew. I feared even more turmoil to come. My thought was to arm students and administrators with water pistols. And have a *'day of insanity'* - allowing everyone to harmlessly let off a little steam.

So, as President of the Student Government, I proposed my idea to the University President. He immediately agreed. Rather than water pistols, he suggested he and I meet on the quad in front of the Student Union. A formal duel.

President to president. Mano a mano. With cream pies.

I immediately accepted and word went out. The press was notified. The news hit the wire services and the event took on a life of its own.

A few days later, we were set to go. *The NY Times, Hartford Courant,* and *Hartford Times* covered it as did the local and regional affiliate stations of CBS, NBC, and ABC. *Life Magazine* sent a reporter and photographer and there were a dozen radio stations describing the action.

Donned in black capes and top hats, we formally marched with our seconds to the ground on which we were to engage in battle. The rules of engagement were recited. Back-to-back we were to march three steps, then turn and fire our pies. Then again at two step, and finally, at one step to ensure we would both be covered in cream pies.

The cream pies were set on the table. A scrum of media along with hundreds of students moved in closer for a better view. I got hit square in the face with his first shot. My first throw went wide. It caught a reporter from a NY TV station staining his fine brown leather jacket.

Throwing a pie with accuracy is more difficult than pitching a baseball. The next shots were a bit of a blur as my vision was impaired with a face full of cream pie. But all of our remaining shots hit their intended target. Our faces were covered in pie. Underneath our creamed faces were a pair of beaming smiles. The entire campus shared a joyful moment.

This event took place a week after the presidential election. The country was looking for a story to feel good about. It was otherwise an extraordinarily slow and depressing news day. Our Pie Duel filled that void.

The Duel made the national news on all three networks, and it was the front-page story in newspapers both locally and nationally. Johnnie Carson mentioned it in his monologue. Photos even appeared in several newspapers in Europe and Japan. My fifteen minutes of fame culminated with a four-page spread in *Life Magazine*. A few years later it even showed up in "Ripley's Believe It or Not."

In the days that followed the Pie Duel, I was about as full of myself as one could be. I felt like I was walking on air. My ego soared.

I stopped into the local supermarket walking with the stride of an invincible young man. As I tossed groceries into the shopping cart, I noticed at the end of the aisle an older couple talking to each other and pointing toward me. With a mountain of confidence, I strode up the aisle and introduced myself.

"Yes, you are right. I was the guy who threw cream pies with the President of the University of Hartford the other day," I said.

"We don't know about that. But young man, you are pushing our cart."

With that, I removed my box of Cap'n Crunch and jar of Skippy Peanut Butter. Properly deflated, I returned their shopping cart and walked meekly away knowing that I had just received a life lesson.

From that day forward, I periodically hear a little voice in my head. *"Schmuck. Don't be such an ass,"* helping me to keep my ego in check.

With University of Hartford President Archibald Woodruff

World Series Tickets

In 1962, the major league baseball expanded. The brand-new New York team was named the New York Metropolitans. A mouthful. So, the name was shortened to the team we know today: *The New York Mets.*

A new stadium was being built in Queens to coincide with the opening of the 1964 New York World's Fair. The Mets played their first two years at the legendary Polo Grounds in upper Manhattan. It was once the home of the New York Giants before they moved to San Francisco, leaving the city without a National League team.

The old ballpark was charming but in need of a wrecking ball, much like the team it fielded. Their new roster comprised a smattering of over-the-hill stars and some minor league players who would never become stars.

The Mets fielded the worst team in the history of baseball. They were terrible. Each day, they found new and laughable ways to lose their games. Dropping fly balls. Not touching bases while running. Throwing to the wrong base. Striking out over and over and over again. Simply put, they were horrible. But loveable and their fan base was loyal.

My uncle Jack took me to their 2nd home game ever. They lost. We laughed. And I became a life-long fan.

With the exception of their 1969 fluke season when, miraculously, they won the World Series. They continued to play worse than mediocre baseball. Until the 1973 when they started to win again. And again.

But this story is not about the Mets. Or baseball. It is about how I scored World Series Tickets in 1973.

That was the year I graduated from college, got married, and moved to NY. I had no job. I spent my days sending out resumes and watching the Watergate hearings on TV. Evenings were spent watching the Mets. Once again, they began winning.

Later that summer, I finally got a job in Manhattan working as an Executive Recruiter. I had a desk in a large open room (called a boiler room) with 20 others making phone calls, trying to convince people to change jobs in order for me to earn a commission. It was called *'head hunting.'* Not sexy. But accurate.

I wasn't very good at it but I became quite skilled at working the phone. I was charming and quick witted. My deep voice made me sound older and wiser, hiding the truth that I was a 22-year-old kid who could barely pay his rent.

As the summer turned to fall, The Mets inched their way up in the standings. The season ended with The Mets winning the National League pennant. They were slated to play the American League champions, the Oakland A's.

I was determined to get to a World Series game, but with no money, it seemed impossible. Tickets were gone almost instantly. Some were being scalped for more than my monthly rent.

I read that the owner of The Mets, M. Donald Grant was an executive with a large Wall Street brokerage house. So why not call him up and say hello. Afterall, I was pretty good on the phone. Nothing to lose.

I waited until noon when I assumed his office would be the quietest. The conversation went pretty much as follows:

Me: "Donald Grant's office, please."

Operator: "One moment."

Secretary: "Mr. Grant's office. How can I help you?"

Me: "Hello. This is Eric Litsky. I'd like to speak with Don."

Secretary: "One Moment, please"

(Thirty seconds later)

Grant: "Hello, this is Donald Grant," he said in a gruff and distracted voice.

Me: "Hi, Don. How ya doing, buddy? This is Eric Litsky. When I sat with you on a flight from Chicago last year you said you'd set aside some tickets if our Mets ever got into the World Series. Well. I'm calling to collect, my friend."

(Note – I never met the man. And I had never been west of

Buffalo. I couldn't believe he didn't hang up the phone).

Grant: "Er. Um. Yes. Sure," he stammered. "I'll put you on with my secretary to make the arrangements."

(Holy crap. I'm going to the World Series. One very long

minute later, she came back on the phone).

Secretary: "Yes, Mr. Litsky. Sorry for the delay. How many tickets would you like, sir?"

Me: "Would four be, ok?"

Secretary: "That would be for each of the home games, right?"

(What the hell).

Me: "Sure. That would be fine."

Secretary: "You do know that we need to charge you. That will be $10 times 4 seats for each of three games. The total is $120. Can you come to our offices this afternoon to pick up the tickets?"

(Where am I going to get $120 from?)

Me: "Yes. I'll send a messenger down from my office"

(That would be me).

I hung up the phone and let out a shout. I was going to the World Series!

Only problem: I had $7 in my pocket. I needed $120 right away. I sold off a pair of the tickets for $60 (3 crisp $20 bills) to my boss. Soon thereafter, he gave me a raise and a promotion. I then scrambled around my office borrowing the rest. All in small denominations.

With the money in my pocket, I headed downtown on the Subway to Wall Street. This was going to be great.

As directed, I rang the bell on an unmarked door in the alley next to Mr. Grant's office building. When I announced that I was Eric Litsky's messenger, I was buzzed in. The clerk had me inspect the three sets of tickets. I was stunned.

These were box seats in the Loge section behind home plate. I did my best to keep a straight face as I laid out the cash. Three crisp $20 bills. Plus $60 dollars of crumpled tens, fives and ones. The clerk gave me a strange look as he counted the cash. He shrugged his shoulders, handed me the tickets, and I was on my way.

Back at my office, I gave my boss his tickets. I could hardly wait for the day to end so I could share my exciting news. I was on my way to the World Series. *My childhood dream!*

That night after dinner, I felt a bit feverish. By bedtime, I was shivering and running a temperature of 103. I came down with the Hong Kong Flu. I spent the next six days in bed with chills, feeling like I was going to die. I slept through every pitch of the World Series broadcasted on our bedside TV. Of course, the Mets lost.

I'd like to think that there is a moral to this story. Something about getting punished for telling a fib. Or misrepresenting facts. I guess it is just a part of the glorious game of baseball where you can expect the unexpected to happen at any time.

The tickets did not go to waste. Two of the games went to my father and brothers. Tickets to the third game went to my Uncle Jack. He introduced me to the NY Mets in their 1962 inaugural season.

My 60-year love affair with this baseball team continues to this day. I have a pair of red seats in my basement playroom from Shea Stadium which was demolished in 2008. And I have several signed baseballs from my favorite Met players displayed in my office. A brick in the walkway to the main entrance to the Met's new home, Citi Field proudly states:

Litsky Family
Loyal Mets Fans since 1962

Thanks, Uncle Jack.

Enter Gate D

15	L	3
SEC.	ROW	SEAT

1973 WORLD SERIES

SHEA STADIUM

GAME

4

ADMIT ONE SUBJECT TO THE CONDITIONS SET FORTH ON BACK HEREOF

RETAIN THIS RAIN CHECK

LOGE RESERVED

Est. Price $9.35
N.Y.S. Tax .65
Total $10.00

NATIONAL LEAGUE vs. AMERICAN LEAGUE

Played under the supervision of COMMISSIONER OF BASEBALL | METROPOLITAN BASEBALL CLUB, INC.—AGENT

1973 WORLD SERIES SHEA STADIUM

RIGHT RESERVED TO REFUND PRICE AND REVOKE LICENSE GRANTED BY THIS TICKET

ADMIT TO

LOGE RESERVED

baseball

GAME

4

Played under the supervision of COMMISSIONER OF BASEBALL

DO NOT DETACH THIS COUPON

Suzuki Violin

My two sons, Jason and Jonathan, were rowdy. And physical. They are fourteen months apart. Each tipped the scales at over 10½ lbs. at birth. They were very big boys. And very, very active.

At four months, Jason crawled up our carpeted staircase. We found his pacifier on the 10th step after he tumbled backwards down the stairs. He never really learned to walk. At seven months, he started running. And didn't stop.

Jonathan was built like a fire hydrant. He also had a ferocious temper. Not a great combination. He often got into trouble at school. On the school bus. And at home. But from a very young age, he displayed a keen sense of humor, developed well beyond his years.

They both excelled at sports which helped to burn off excess energy. But I was equally concerned with their intellectual development.

Clearly, these boys were bright, but it was hard to keep them focused. I wanted something for them which would not necessarily come easy, and with a little hard work, they could make quantifiable progress. Perhaps even translate that accomplishment into achieving other challenging things later in life.

My thought was Suzuki Violin.

I rented two half-sized violins, signed them up for lessons, and hoped for the best.

I cannot remember what I bribed them with to get them to their first lesson, but I got them there. Suzuki success requires active parental involvement with a few minutes of practice each night.

I had some musical experience, so I rented a violin too, and tried to learn along with my boys. Our teacher possessed an abundance of patience. Somehow, she was able to keep the boys from fencing with their violin bows. Or swatting a nerf ball with their violins.

No doubt neither would become a Joshua Bell. Or Itzhak Perlman. But I thought if you could play the violin a little bit, you could do just about anything.

At five and six years old, the prospect of scratching out a simple tune may have been a bridge too far.

As the weeks and months passed, our playing became slightly more recognizable. Our teacher asked if we would participate in a year-end Suzuki recital the following Sunday. Mother's Day. It was to be held in the church of a private school close to our home.

I agreed.

I assumed there would be a dozen of her students plus some parents. But when we showed up it was standing room only in a 300-seat church. This recital included Suzuki students from throughout the region. On each side of the pews, parents and grandparents plugged in their video recorders. There were cameras everywhere.

The first two rows in the front pews had masking tape running across the seat backs with each participant's name directing us where to sit. I discovered that I was the only student there over 12 years of age. I felt 300 sets of eyes staring at the back of my head, leaving the audience to wonder who the big shmuck with the mustache was. I faced forward in silent prayer. It was a church, after all. I prayed for a power outage so we could get the hell out of there. Maybe I could salvage some dignity.

Toward the end of the program, our teacher introduced us. She had nice words to say about parental commitment and how the three of us were learning how to play together. Our piece for the afternoon was "Twinkle, Twinkle, Little Star" in the tricky bowing rhythm she called "Mississippi Hot Dog."

With that introduction, we held up our violins and in our best posture, we proceeded with reckless abandon. The only note we played in unison was the first. We were horrible. Mercifully, it ended quickly. We received a nice ovation. More like pity clapping.

Jason and I gave an appropriate head bow to the audience, but Jonathan brought down the house with a heroic bow as if he had just performed a Vivaldi concerto at Carnegie Hall. Even at age five, he knew how to work a crowd. And work the crowd he did.

We then packed up our instruments and went back to our lives.

Never to play violin again.

Trying to coax Jonathan and Jason to violin lessons

On Parenting

I was far from a perfect father. I tried hard, but I was just a kid myself. Becoming a first-time parent at age 25, floundering in my first marriage, struggling financially. New career. New home. A bone-crunching mortgage. A year later we had a second child.

My wife and I stayed overwhelmed for the decade that followed. Our marriage was over shortly thereafter. What I did well or not so well is a story for my children to tell. I am too close to be objective.

That said, I thought I'd take a look at how my parents did by sharing two extraordinary examples, one of great parenting, which had a profound influence on my life, and one astonishingly poor, leaving me to wonder how I survived their parenting.

Cambria Heights, in my earliest days, was a mostly white lower middle-class Queens neighborhood. It was unusual to see a person of color. As the years passed, the neighborhood and its schools became increasingly more diverse. But in the late 1950s it was *"Lily White."*

My parents had the foresight to expose my brother Andy and me to a diverse environment. To experience other races and cultures from a very young age, they sent us to summer camps run by several different Settlement Houses from the Lower East Side of Manhattan.

A century earlier, Settlement Houses established the idea that immigrants and low-income families deserved basic services, quality education, decent housing, and access to open space for exercise and health. A 250-acre estate was donated to University Settlement and a summer camp was opened there. This was my first summer camp experience. I was seven. My brother was nine.

The camp was located in Beacon, NY, 60 miles north of the city. It was the first time I experienced outdoor space on a grand scale. My new friends were Black, Puerto Rican, and Chinese. I don't remember if there were any other White kids in my bunk. We were just kids enjoying summer together.

Pete Seeger, the famous folk singer who roamed the country with Woody Guthrie ("This Land Is Your Land") during the Great Depression, had a home nearby. He often came over with his banjo, teaching us young campers to sing some of the well-known folk songs he wrote including "If I Had a Hammer" and "Where Have All the Flowers Gone?" This was the very beginnings of The Civil Rights Movement. With arms around each other, he'd lead us in the old spiritual he made famous the world over, "We Shall Overcome."

We just called him Pete.

I attended Settlement House summer camps for the next seven years. The experience engrained in me at a very young age that we are all God's children. I've done my best to teach that to my children. And to my grandchildren.

This was the gift my parents gave me. It was a remarkable feat of good parenting, particularly when you consider the slowly evolving attitudes of the 1950s and 1960s. It was the early years of the civil rights and antiwar movements.

Like all parents, mine made their share of mistakes. When I was four years-old, they lost me in Manhattan for an afternoon. At 10, I babysat for my five-year-old sister and infant brother. Today, Child Services would have removed us from our home. At 14, they left me and my 16-year-old brother home alone over the New Year's weekend when they took our younger siblings away for the holiday weekend. My stomach still churns when I see a bottle of Southern Comfort. And they let us purchase a $35 car that was a death trap on wheels.

But I think their worst parenting decision was letting me go with five high school buddies to Washington D.C. a couple of days after the riots, looting, and fires following the assassination of Martin Luther King Jr.

Dr. King was killed on Friday, April 4, 1968. It was a horrible event made worse by the rioting afterwards. More than 1,200 separate fires blazed in riot-torn DC.

Stores were looted. Neighborhoods devastated. Eventually some 14,000 National Guard troops were called in to quell the upheaval, a larger military force than the one that occupied the Capital during the Civil War.

Among the 100 cities that experienced rioting after Dr. King's assassination, Washington DC was arguably the most devastating.

My friends and I landed at National Airport (now Reagan) a few days after the worst of the riots. The smell of smoke from charred buildings lingered in the air. We cabbed over to our hotel at DuPont Circle past scores of military vehicles. Armed soldiers patrolled the streets.

It never occurred to us that being here at this time was a terrible idea. The hotel was glad for our business. They were mostly vacant and happy to give us adjoining rooms on an empty floor. Normally, Washington would be packed full of springtime tourists. This weekend, it was eerily quiet.

We had the city to ourselves. Half a dozen 17-year-olds. On our own without supervision in a city that was just recovering from devastating riots.

We acted like any group of teenagers left to their own devices. We horsed around, smoked, played cards late into the night, tossed firecrackers, and had a water fight that soaked our rooms. We posed for photos with National Guard soldiers in front of the White

House. They let us wear their helmets and sit in their jeep but wouldn't let us hold their guns. We were oblivious to everything around us. Just kids acting out of control for three fun-filled days. We were immature and lacked the social consciousness to understand the significance of Dr. King's life and work. That would come to each of us later.

I still get together with some of those guys. We are now all parents. And grandparents. We reminisce about that weekend in DC and shake our heads as one of us would inevitably ask:

"What the hell were our parents thinking?"

Back row – Stuart, George and me.

Front row – Mike, Arnie, Bob and Frank .

Life As a Single Dad

Divorce is gut-wrenching. Time consuming. Expensive. Everybody loses. Except for the attorneys. The best you can hope for is to end the marriage with as little pain as possible. Mine was no different, except that I ended up with the house and the kids. Unusual in 1989.

I was close to broke raising two kids, trying to find a solid footing. *Terra Firma, to begin a new life.*

I thought it might be good to spend some quality, one-on-one time with each of my boys and open them up to a new cultural experience.

I took Jason, who was twelve, to the Hartford Symphony. He liked it. There is nothing more impressive than hearing an 80-piece symphonic orchestra performance. I did not suggest that most of the violin section likely began with Suzuki lessons (see my 'Suzuki Violin' story).

My eleven-year-old, Jonathan, came with me to the theater. It was an Avant Garde production of some edgy European drama. We had front row seats.

The second act opened with the two lead characters waking up in their marital bed. The covers flew off. They stood up stark naked. Their dialogue continued as they got dressed. Ever so slowly.

Jonathan leaned over and said in too loud a voice, "I like the theater,

Dad. Thanks." Those within an earshot burst out laughing. I'm not sure if the performers heard any of it. But the show continued with my son hoping for another nude scene.

All he could talk about to his friends was how I took him to see naked people on stage. I tried to add a little culture to his life. But his friends, and probably their parents, thought I took him to a strip club.

I've never been a fan of Halloween. That first week in November is hell if you happen to have a school bus stop in front of your house. Which we did. The neighborhood kids would consume huge amounts of Halloween candy. The sugar highs often resulted in bus stop fights.

Time to take a stand.

The next Halloween, I took myself to a Job Lot store. But instead of buying large bags of candy, I purchased 125 toothbrushes. There are a lot of children in our neighborhood.

Surprisingly, the little ones who trick-or-treated at my home shrieked in delight at getting a new toothbrush. This was a big deal for them. There was a mixed reaction among the other kids. I heard an occasional "asshole and shithead" as the 9 and 10-year-olds strode away from my door and down the walkway.

My boys were humiliated. When their school mates asked if their dad really handed out toothbrushes for Halloween, they lied and said it was the guy next door.

I recently bumped into a young woman who grew up with my kids. She was now in her 40's with a pre-teen of her own. She said she remembered the Halloween toothbrushes. At the time, she thought I was crazy. But now as an adult, she thinks about it each Halloween and sees the wisdom of my action. I asked if she would ever do that.

"You *must* be crazy," she said.

My ex-wife and I came to terms in our divorce. Time to split up our stuff. All I really wanted was to keep the house and the kids. She could have whatever she wanted so long as the boys' rooms were left intact.

The week she was to move out the belongings, I took the boys on a long road trip.... a little 'guy' time on the road. Off we went to the Baseball Hall of Fame. Niagara Falls. Toronto. West Point. And then to visit my parents on Long Island. Six days on the road.

An ungodly number of NY Thruway miles, but a good time to bond and just hang out together. What made it particularly long was that a tape got stuck in my 8-year-old Subaru. I was unable to eject it. Over and over and over again. Gloria Gaynor singing "I Will Survive." No other music. And no working radio.

We headed home from our six-day trek. Not sure of what to expect, I opened the door to a house that was largely empty. The boys' rooms were just as they had left them six days earlier.

Our voices echoed in the mainly empty home now cavernous without much furniture. So, we hopped back in the car and went out for a large Pizza with extra cheese.

Once again, the tape played "I Will Survive."

And I did.

Not Yet

I felt a sharp pinching pain in the center of my chest. It was like a muscle spasm increasing in intensity. The pain intensified. I felt like I was being ripped apart, as if some horrible beast had dug its claws into each side of my chest, pulling at my rib cage to separate it.

A few moments later, I began to perspire. It was a cool afternoon, early October, but I was sweating like it was a mid-August heat wave. The pain in my chest increased in its intensity so I thought I should have it checked out at the walk-in medical center I jokingly refer to as the "Doc in the box." The pain was too much for me to handle driving, so I asked my neighbor.

It's a 15-minute ride to the walk-in center. He drove it in 10. As he sped down the tree-lined streets of suburban Simsbury, CT, my condition rapidly deteriorated. Definitely a muscle spasm, I thought. A quick shot of something and I'd be on my way. Thirty seconds was all the doctor needed to determine that I was having a heart attack.

Five minutes later, I was rolled out through the waiting room into an ambulance. This was my second ambulance ride this year. My son, Jonathan, hurt his neck diving off the high board at the town swimming pool earlier that summer. After a few terrifying hours, he walked out of the trauma center. I hoped my ambulance ride would have the same happy ending.

It is a twenty-minute ride from the walk-in clinic to John Dempsey Hospital, a teaching hospital of the University of Connecticut School of Medicine.

Two EMT's were riding with me. One gave me several hits of morphine to dull the pain. It did not. He then took a medical history, probing to discover how a seemingly healthy 37-year-old has a heart attack. The other placed small suction cups on my chest and legs which were in turn connected to a series of multi-colored wires running to a portable EKG (electro-cardiogram).

They radioed in the results along with my vital signs, pulse, blood pressure, and temperature. No one looked me in the eyes other than to determine the dilation of my pupils. I felt completely disconnected from the reality of this experience.

To distract myself from my pain, I tried to figure out the route we were taking by viewing lamp posts and treetops through the small square windows in the ambulance's rear door. All I could really determine was that we were moving very fast. The siren screamed as we weaved through traffic.

My thoughts went to Jimmy Porter, a childhood friend from my old neighborhood. I hadn't thought about him in decades. I remember Jimmy telling me that you should say a little prayer when you hear an ambulance. I hoped someone out there was saying a little prayer for me, rather than bitching about moving to the side of the road to let my ambulance fly by.

When we hit the emergency room doors, the sights and sounds got blurry. A blonde-haired nurse, whose name I never learned, took my hand. She looked me square in the face and told me in a soothing voice to stay with her.

"Hang in there. You'll be OK."

I remember that she had smooth hands and wore a small diamond engagement ring on her left hand. Her trusting green eyes helped to keep me from panicking.

The events of this moment were out of my control. I knew I was in really big trouble. I had to trust that the good people in this room would not let me die. It was the feeling of falling backwards off a tall ladder hoping that someone would be there to catch me. I willed myself to relax and let go of control. Letting go of control was never something I was particularly good at. Clearly, I was not in control of any part of this moment.

As I was wheeled quickly on a gurney from the ambulance into the emergency room, I could see flashes of the greens and blues of the gowns worn by the doctors and nurses. Mainly my view was of the acoustical ceiling tiles and the florescent overhead lighting. There were doctors everywhere. This is a teaching hospital filled with students and residents, each wanting to experience my fucking heart attack.

On the count of three, I was lifted off the gurney and dropped on to the examining table like a sack of potatoes. I hadn't been lifted up since I was a child.

A doctor, whose bedside manner was firm and serious, almost gruff, replaced the nurse who earlier held my hand. I was poked and prodded, connected to machines to monitor my vital signs. The zigzagging lines on the monitors spoke in a language only a physician could understand. The good news for me was that none of the lines were flat.

The machines continued to beep. IV lines were placed in my left arm and blood was drawn from my right arm. Everyone in the room had a piece of me. The pain in my chest worsened. I could feel my eyes fill with tears. The room got blurry. Everyone seemed to be moving in slow motion. I could make out sporadic phrases like 'crashing,' 'losing him' and 'stat.'

Finally, I could take no more of the pain. Or of the fright. I closed my eyes in hopes that I could escape. In my "mind's eye" I saw a large door suspended in mid- air about three feet above me.

I reached up to open it. Inside was a puffy, cloudy, peaceful place glowing in surrealistic bright white light. I peered inside. In an instant my pain was gone. I never thought much about heaven. Or for that matter anything mystical or religious. Yet somehow, I knew that if I closed that door behind me, my pain would be gone.

Forever. And I would not be coming back.

More than a place, it was a feeling. A feeling of ecstasy. Of pure love. How does one describe a feeling of being bathed in total love? An invisible energy swept over my entire body, gently cradling me. I could feel it. But could not see it. In that moment, I was completely at peace. I was no longer frightened. And no longer in pain. Just then, I heard a voice loudly inside of my head.

It said in a forceful voice, "Not Yet."

In an instant, I snapped back into the reality of being on the emergency room gurney, once again in terrible pain. I heard one of the doctors say something like "he's back." A woman's voice said, "Thank God." I saw someone put away the defibrillation paddles. I assume I must have coded.

They gave me an experimental clot buster called TPA. State of the Art for the day. In an hour or so my pain subsided. The hectic activity in the emergency room gradually diminished. The blood tests determined that I had indeed had a myocardial infarction. A heart attack. I was absolutely stunned.

The last time I was a hospital patient was 37 years earlier. Bronx Hospital. The day I was born. That began one adventure, this was to be the beginning of another.

The vision of the door and the bliss behind it may have lasted only a few moments, but it would go on to change my life forever. It took many months before I could talk about what happened on that gurney. I had had a "near death experience."

For the next two weeks, I watched the leaves outside my hospital window turn from green to the brilliant oranges, yellows, and reds of a bright New England autumn. Soon, those leaves would drop. Trees would lay dormant, awaiting new life in the spring. In that moment, it was the metaphor of my life.

I had many hours to contemplate how my life took such a weird and frightening turn. I committed to get myself into better physical shape, consume a healthier diet. Intuitively, I knew I needed to put more love in my life.

After six weeks of cardio rehab, I was ready to start moving on with my life. The question was, "How to begin?" It was now the holiday season.

Christmas had been my favorite time of year. My ex-wife is an Italian-Catholic girl. What a joyous time full of love and sharing. Each year after the birth of our two boys, our celebration of the Christmas season grew larger and larger. But I lost Christmas in the divorce earlier that year.

Afterall, I am Jewish. So that seemed fair. Facing the prospect of being alone during the holiday season, I had an inspiration. I would become Santa Claus. A Jewish Santa. Why the hell not?

For the next several years, I was the official Santa of John Dempsey Hospital. A little payback to the place and the staff that saved my life. I roamed the corridors with my melodious and jolly Ho! Ho! Ho!

I loved every moment I was there.

I then put the word out that I was available to make house calls as Santa. The deal was simple. I would make a Santa stop. You make a special contribution to the charity of *your* choosing. My only payment was the joy that came back tenfold in smiles, laughter, and hugs. It helped to heal my heart.

In the years that followed, I visited dozens and dozens of families. Children, parents, and even grandparents shared a moment sitting on my lap. Laughing. And having their pictures taken.

We'd sing a song or two and I'd be out the door before anyone wondered aloud why I appeared from a Toyota in the driveway rather than from a sleigh on the roof.

I have no idea how much money was raised for these good causes. More importantly, was the good feelings derived from making those donations and the joy of spending some holiday time with their very own Jewish Santa.

Years later, I fell in love with and eventually married Norma. We incorporated her family Christmas traditions into the life we share. As time went by, I no longer needed to fill the void in my life by being Santa. My heart is now full of love.

Santa still visits my home each Christmas to the delight of my children and grandchildren.

And I get to be in every photo.

With granddaughter, Emerson, on her first Christmas

In Search of My Higher Self

So, I recovered from a heart attack which nearly did me in. Now I was left to figure out what the hell happened. I was 37. I could not shake the image of the doorway that hovered over my gurney in the ER that day. Did I really see another dimension just out of arms reach? Or was I just crazy? I couldn't shake it. Or explain it. I know I was engulfed by a force of some kind. Best explanation was to call it pure love.

I had a "near death experience."

I had never been a mystical or religious person, so I had trouble talking about this. I didn't have the vocabulary, but I needed to understand it as a part of my healing process.

This led me on a 10-year journey inward, interacting and learning from dozens of teachers from many different disciplines. I was determined to become more enlightened.

My first teacher was Ram Das, a best-selling author and lecturer on Hinduism and mindfulness meditation. His "Be Here Now" is a classic in New Age literature. I spent two weeks with him at The Omega Institute in Rhinebeck, NY, and in the Virgin Islands. We became friendly. He pointed me in a number of directions to explore my personal spiritual path.

And so, it began.

I studied the ancient Jewish Mystical teachings of the Kabala with

Orthodox Rabbis, and I spent three days in classes with the Dalai Lama studying Tibetan Buddhism.

I was formally named in Sweat Lodge by an Oglala Sioux medicine man, and I spun with Whirling Dervishes, Sufi followers of the teachings of the 13th century Muslim mystic, Rumi.

Moving my body led me to study Tai Chi with Master Al Haung, sensitizing me to the movement of energy (Chi) through my body. I took classes in reflexology and completed level 1 Reiki training, a healing modality. I got regular body work to open my energy systems and unblock stresses I was holding.

My travels took me to Machu Picchu, the lost city of the Incas in the Peruvian Andes; Chichen Itza, Tulum and Uxmal, Mayan ruins in the Mexican Yucatan; and to Haleakala high above the Hawaiian Island of Maui. I slept under the stars in the High Sierras of California and in the Utah desert.

For several years, I studied with a Psychic working on developing my personal intuitive skills. I experimented with channeling spirit guides and engaged in several past life regressions.

The channeling led me to spend a week with Barbara Marciniak. She authored many books on her contact with (ET) entities from the Pleiades, a cluster of seven sister stars the subject of myths and legends in many cultures.

During this time, I devoured scores of books from the New Age section of the bookstore and read through many sacred texts including *Book of Mormon*, *The Koran*, *The Bible*, and *The Keys of Enoch*.

My decade long quest for spiritual enlightenment was exhilarating and intellectually stimulating. But it was also exhausting. There was simply too much to learn and experience in one lifetime. I finally came to the realization that I was barely skimming the surface. My search for higher meaning brought me back to the words of my first spiritual teacher: Ram Das.

I made a conscious decision for myself to simply "Be Here Now."

I no longer need to know what the future brings. I do not have the wisdom or the intellect to understand where we came from or where we are headed.

For me, I will continue to be the best man I can be, living out my remaining days with a heart full of love, firmly planted in the present. And to simply "Be Here Now."

With Ram Das who taught me to 'Be Here Now.'

Da Capital

When asked what DC stood for in Washington DC, I once heard someone say:

"Da Capital."

Norma and I had been dating for several months. It was an exciting time for her. New relationship. Soon to be formally divorced, and though she had been living in the U.S. for decades, she had just recently become a U.S. Citizen.

To celebrate her status as a newly minted citizen, we scheduled a weekend in our nation's capital. I knew Washington well, having visited there many times. My older brother Andy also has been living in DC for many years. It was a good time to have a visit and show off my new girlfriend.

Saying girlfriend when you are a middle-aged man sounds creepy, like you are dating a high school girl. I assure you that Norma, though younger than me, was well past her teenage years. So, girlfriend it was.

I called our local Congressional office and told an aide that I am bringing a "new" American to DC for the first time. I asked if it would be possible to get a tour of the Capitol building. It was scheduled for the afternoon of our Friday arrival.

It was a beautiful afternoon in early September when we arrived at Washington National Airport. I refuse to call it Reagan as the airport was already named after a president. The first one.

After checking in to our hotel, the first hotel night of our new relationship, we cabbed over to the Capitol for our Friday afternoon tour. Congress was not in session, so the magnificent building was eerily quiet. We hit it off with our tour guide who enjoyed our enthusiasm about the building and its rich history.

Since it was quiet, he took us onto the floor of Congress where we continued chatting in the seats usually reserved for the Supreme Court Justices during the State of The Union Address.

We then strolled to the Senate side of the Capitol building and walked into the Senate Chamber (also called the Well), the very room where the Senate has debated the life altering issues of the day since it opened just prior to the Civil War. The nation's 100 senators sit at individual desks arranged on a tiered semicircular platform facing the rostrum. Norma momentarily lost her balance while looking up at the extraordinary dome and touched one of the desks. A Capitol Policeman sternly warned her not to touch anything. This was a serious place.

Walking out, our guide asked if we wanted to see something really cool. "Sure," we immediately answered in unison. Upstairs to the Speaker of House's office we went. He exchanged a few words with the security officer and the doors were opened to the office of the Speaker, Dennis Hastert.

Hastert resigned in disgrace. He was convicted of paying hush money to cover up crimes of child molestation prior to being elected to public office. He was the highest-ranking elected official in U.S. history to serve a prison sentence.

At the rear of the office is the Speaker's Balcony. I remember seeing it on my television once every four years as it sits high above the presidential Inaugural platform.

Out we went to experience a view few seldom do. As we looked below and out onto the Mall, I imagined the Speakers who sat here and contemplated solutions to the issues of their day.....war, slavery, civil rights, impeachment, taxes and a thousand other pressing matters impacting the lives of all Americans.

My brother, who was involved in local Washington politics for decades, was flabbergasted that we were invited in to places he had never seen.

The next day, we visited the Vietnam War Memorial, two 245-foot-long black granite walls etched with the names of the 58,220 service men and women who lost their lives in the conflict. The walls are sunken into the ground. They meet at a height of 10 ft and then taper to less than a foot at their ends. The walk along the wall from sunshine into shadow and then back to brightness over the span of nearly 500 ft., has a powerful visceral effect. Many are brought to tears as they exit the memorial. Norma and I were no exception.

Just across Constitution Ave from the Memorial is the National Academy of Sciences Building. A 12 ft bronze statue of a seated and smiling Albert Einstein graces its entrance. At Andy's suggestion, Norma and I crawled up onto Einstein's lap. Being caressed by Mr. Einstein went a long way toward healing the emotional pain the Vietnam War Memorial inflicted on our psyche.

After dinner, Andy took us on his nighttime tour of the Monuments. As spectacular as they are in daylight, these imposing monuments are infinitely more beautiful when they are lit up at night.

As we made our way around town, we noticed the lights on The White House were extinguished. In his 30 years of living here, Andy had never seen it dark.

The last stop on our tour was the Lincoln Memorial. It was late and the crowds were long gone. We walked up the steps and stood for a moment on the very spot Dr. King delivered his "I Have a Dream" speech many years ago.

The space inside the neoclassical temple which houses the large statue of a seated Abe Lincoln was empty. As Norma read the inscription of his Gettysburg address etched on the wall, Andy and

I hid behind one of the Doric pillars.....leaving her alone with Mr. Lincoln in this spectacular space. Now that is what I call a gigantic welcome for any new citizen.

We flew home early on Sunday morning. I noticed security tighter at the airport but thought it was my imagination. I've got to stop reading so many spy novels.

Norma and I thoroughly enjoyed our time in DC and our first weekend away together as a couple. She was so proud to be a citizen. It is hard to not be a proud American after such a weekend in Washington.

On Tuesday morning, two planes struck and destroyed the World Trade Center towers in Lower Manhattan. Another hit the Pentagon and a fourth was brought down by heroic passengers in a field in Pennsylvania.

The world has not been the same since.

The Speaker's Balcony

Vieques

I fell in love with my wife at a whore house. I should explain. A dozen years after my divorce, I met a beautiful woman named Norma. We really hit it off so, we decided to take a vacation together in the Caribbean.

I had read about the beauty of the island of Vieques, a crescent-shaped island off the coast of Puerto Rico. I was eager to kayak in its famous bioluminescent bay where on a moonless night the water looks like liquid gold.

Vieques was long the home of a large US Navy base. It had recently been shuttered after many years of anti-Navy demonstrations. A friend suggested we stay at a lovely spot on the island called Bananas.

From San Juan, we took a cab across the island to Fajardo, arriving just in time for the afternoon ferry to Vieques. Neither of us read the small print on the flyer. It warned that the seas can be rough. It suggested taking motion sickness medicine an hour before boarding.

It was a beautiful day to sit up top and enjoy the hour-long ferry ride. To this day, my stomach still gets a bit queasy remembering that trip. Ten minutes out and the ferry rocked and rolled on the choppy seas. By the time we arrived in Vieques, our skin was a light shade of green. We were wobbly kneed, barely able to hold down our breakfasts.

Once on Vieques, we directed a taxi to take us to Bananas.

Bananas was basically an open-air beach bar. Attached was a restaurant and some rooms down a dingy hallway behind the bar. We paid cash in advance for the room. Too sick to question or argue or to ask to see the room first, we gladly paid so we could have a place to lay down.

We were escorted down the dark hallway to one of the dozen rooms. We paid $10 per night extra for the room with air conditioning. The bartender opened the door to our room. Our jaws dropped. But not in a good way.

The room was constructed from compressed wood. Unfinished. No paint. No stain. No carpet. The floor was exposed plywood as was the queen-sized bed frame that sat prominently in the middle of the room. There were no windows.

Where was the "lovely outdoor sitting area off the well-appointed bedroom" as advertised in their brochure? The bartender then threw open a double door in the back of the room to the screened in porch. It faced the overflowing garbage cans in the rear of the kitchen where a busboy in a soiled apron was taking his smoke break. A couple of roosters scampered across the trash filled yard. They would wake us up at the crack of dawn for the next three mornings.

We were still too nauseous from the ferry ride to kick up a fuss, and frankly, a little embarrassed that we had just paid for four nights. In cash. In advance. This had to be the worst motel room either of us could have imagined.

My experience with women had been that I'd get blamed for a disaster like this horrible place. Or at least there would be a huge fight, frustrated that our first romantic getaway was ruined.

But that was not to be. Though we were both really unhappy, neither of us placed blame on the other. No fight. No angry words. We just decided to make the best of it. It was at that moment I knew

I wanted this woman in my life forever.

Norma and I married some years later. We have stayed in many hotels around the world. Some good. Some not so good. But none could compare to this experience. Now when we come upon a place to stay that is really crappy, we simply remind ourselves that it is, after all, "Better than Bananas."

It occurred to us that Bananas probably served as a whore house when the US Navy had a large base on the island.

So, I guess you could say, I fell in love with my wife at an old whore house on the tropical Island of Vieques.

Many years later, Hurricane Maria destroyed Bananas. It has since been rebuilt. From its website, it looks like a nice place. But memories of the original dump will forever warm my heart.

Red, White, and Green

Old women dressed in filthy, ragged clothing selling small boxes of Chicklets and cheap blankets to passing tourists. The city was loud, dirty and dangerous. Trapped in dismal poverty. Tijuana. That was the only Mexico I knew.

That is until I met Norma. She would eventually become my wife.

On our first date, I detected a slight accent. I couldn't quite place it. Her light complexion. Green eyes. European features. I guessed Czech. I was wrong by an ocean and a half.

She is Mexican. Born and raised in Mexico City.

I shared with her that I had been to Tijuana and hated it.

"Judging Mexico from a few hours in Tijuana is like spending an afternoon in Newark thinking you've seen the U.S."

Fair point. The only thing I hate more than being ignorant is being embarrassed when I get called out on it. I was intrigued with the notion of learning something about a new culture. And I found her to be smoking hot. Twenty years later, I still do.

A few dates later, Norma invited me to celebrate New Year's Eve. Her brother and his family were visiting from Mexico. They were warm, inviting, and fun loving, which in my experience is pretty much the default setting of most Mexicans. Except for those portrayed in Hollywood movies and American TV. I could not have felt more at home.

A Mexican New Year's Eve celebration incorporates many

wonderful traditions. And superstitions. We brought in the New Year by making a wish on each of a dozen grapes we ate at midnight. We then grabbed a broom and took turns symbolically sweeping the bad energy out of the home. We each ran in and out of the house numerous times with suitcases in hand. For a year of travel. And we tossed loose change out of the door for a year of prosperity.

It went on and on, each of us in turn taking part in one tradition after another in joyous laughter as we sipped our tequila into the small hours.

Red underwear is worn for a year of love. Wear something yellow for a year of good fortune. They all spoke English, though my high school Spanish improved with each tequila.

Norma and I have since traveled together to Mexico numerous times. From the sunny beaches of the Mayan Riviera to the sites and tastes of Mexico City. Our travels have taken us to small towns and larger cities and into the hills north of Mexico City. We've explored and pondered the mysteries of the ancient ruins of the Mayans and Aztecs.

We attended a bullfight in Puerto Vallarta, enjoying the pageantry of the opening procession. The sound from the bugles filled the air as the costumed *matadors* and *picadors* entered to rousing applause. But it was all downhill after that. The bull didn't have a chance.

We found ourselves rooting for the bull. Good that we left early.

But what I enjoy most about Mexico is the warmth and kindness of its people.

My first trip to meet Norma's family was the celebration of her mother's 90th birthday. Her mother was beautiful. Sharp as a tack. She was multi-lingual, reading novels in Spanish, French and English. Her home had many oil paintings she created in her younger years. She had a wonderful sense of humor. At 90, she still played poker and the piano.

In my attempt to win her over, I wished her a *feliz cumple anos*. I thought it was happy birthday. Sadly, I wished her a happy rectum. Everyone laughed, making me the butt (pun intended) of the laughter.

There is a tilde over the n which changes the pronunciation from *anos to anyos*. Oops. My bad. But she just smiled, appreciating my effort, lame as it was.

I was able to steal away a few minutes alone with her. I told her that I loved her daughter and she could count on me to take care of her and the children. She paused for a long moment. Stared into my eyes. I wondered what was going through her head. She was a very religious woman who went to church almost every day of her life. Standing in front of her may have been the only Jew to ever set foot in her home. What could she be thinking?

In what might have been a question or a statement, she said, "You are a good man."

"Yes, I try to be," I replied.

She smiled and gave me a nod as others entered the room. That was her acceptance. She passed away before Norma and I were married. It is said that if you want to see what your bride will be like in the future, take a good look at her mother. I am indeed a very lucky man.

Mexican families can be very, very large. Norma has roughly 75 first cousins spread out around the world. I have six. Her cousins have children. Many have grandchildren. The family numbers over a thousand.

We attended the wedding of one of Norma's nephews in the beautiful hill town of San Miguel de Allende, a 3-hour drive from Mexico City. The ceremony took place in a huge historic 17th century Church…. dwarfing every other structure in town. The party was held at a Hacienda. More than six hundred of us celebrated with "white glove service" under the biggest tent I've ever seen. And I've been to the circus.

A very large family, indeed.

Melding my Jewish family with her Mexican family came fairly easy to both of us. We are all about tradition. Love. Laughter. And of course, food.

Our vocabulary is peppered with words and expressions in both Yiddish and Spanish, adding a delightful texture to our communication. We've created new Yiddish/Spanish expressions by combining the languages. My personal favorite is *'Muchas Nachas'* – wishing someone much happiness.

My family now toasts special events with shots of tequila, far superior to the sickeningly sweet concord grape wine we Jews have suffered through for generations.

Norma and I were married in Mexico, bringing our families together with a weeklong party at a small all-inclusive hotel in Cancun.

We arrived as two families. We left as one.

And I am as proud of the Red, White and Green. As I am of the Red, White and Blue.

The Coffee Man

He was the only person I've ever met who was universally loved by all. He stood no more than 5' 6," weighed in at 140 lbs., dripping wet, with piercing blue eyes and a smile that could melt the hardest of hearts. He was my father's older brother, my uncle Morris.

Born to an immigrant family on the eve of World War I, he shared their five-room cold water flat on Manhattan's Lower East Side with his three siblings and my paternal grandparents. On hot days, he liked to sleep on the fire escape where he could catch bits of breeze laden with the lingering odors from the fish market a few doors down on Chrystie Street.

The broken promise of living on a street paved with gold must have been a crushing disappointment to his parents in this overcrowded immigrant neighborhood packed with pushcarts and horse drawn carriages. But it was a vast improvement from the violence of the pogroms of the Russian village of Slonim from where they emigrated.

Though English was taught in the three-story brick schoolhouse on Rivington Street, Yiddish was the language of the neighborhood. And his home.

Morris was gentle and soft spoken. These traits he would carry through adolescence and into adulthood and old age. Beginning at the age of 12, he made daily entries into his diary. For the next 78 years, each day of his life was recorded. Through his eyes, it is the story of our family through most of the 20th century in volumes that take up over eight feet of shelf space.

Morris had a great ear and could mimic the idiosyncrasies of myriad of neighborhood characters. He dabbled performing in the Yiddish theater, but his acting career was cut short when his father became ill. He became the bread winner of the family, delivering telegrams for Western Union until he joined the Army at the start of WWII.

In June 1944, the diminutive Corporal Litsky was in the first wave to hit the beachfront at Normandy in the D-Day Invasion. With 50 lbs. of dynamite (one third of his body weight) strapped to his back, the doors of the Higgins landing craft fell open.

He found himself in neck deep water wading to shore amid a torrent of machine gun fire and too many soldiers to count floating face down in the blood-stained water. Miraculously, he slowly crawled up the beach to safety reciting what childhood prayers he could remember as his ears ached from the din of the battle.

His sergeant knew Morris spoke Yiddish, so he had him interrogate the German POWs. Linguistically, German is a cousin to Yiddish. Imagine the horror as these tall blonde Arian warriors got interrogated by my pint-sized Jewish uncle.

Morris was later wounded and spent the remainder of the war working in the Army post office in Paris. There he became fluent in French. He developed a very close relationship to the Jewish family with whom he lived. Somehow, they had managed to survive the German occupation of the City of Lights.

As the war wound down, they gave Morris a Yellow Star of David with the word *Juif* (French for Jewish) embossed in its center. This identified the wearer as a Jew. The penalty for a Jew not wearing the *Juif* Star of David was a one-way ticket to the death camps. It is ingrained in the soul of Jewish people to "never forget" the horror of the holocaust. Morris' *Juif* Star of David is now in a frame on the wall in my brother Tom's home.

When the war ended, Morris returned to NYC and went to work in his uncle Benny's notion store in Spanish Harlem. He loved talking to customers who were mostly Spanish speaking. In addition to Yiddish, English, and French, he rapidly became fluent in Spanish as well.

When my parents moved Andy and I from the small apartment in the Bronx above my (maternal) grandparent's home to Queens in the early 1950s, Morris moved in.

Morris was my grandparent's tenant and upstairs neighbor for the next 25 years.

At our weekly visits to my grandparents, Andy and me and later our younger siblings, Amy and Tom, were delighted when we found Morris at home. His home was a living museum of our family history. There was a story behind every photo and every collectible that was lovingly displayed on every inch of wall space.

He would delight us with stories of our ancestors from Russia and from his childhood. And, if we asked nicely, he would read from his diary about the day we were born. Or when our parents were married. Or of the Lower East Side. Or of D-Day. Or of Paris. He brought the world closer to home. And we hung on every word.

Morris was a great entertainer. A simple prop like a dish cloth was all that he needed. Tucked in his pants, he was a fat German baker. Draped over his arm he was a snooty French waiter. Wrapped over his head and he became an old Jewish lady. And worn like a bib he became an angry Drill Sergeant.

This collection of characters was intermingled creating a complicated story line told in multiple languages and dialects. It was hysterical and completely original. With some guidance, he might have found his way back to the stage or to television. He certainly had talent.

But Morris was content selling notions, thread, and buttons at his uncle Benny's store.

When my grandparents sold their Bronx home and moved to Great Neck on Long Island to be closer to my parents, Morris followed.

He rented a small apartment close to the LIRR station allowing for easy transportation to his favorite place on the planet, Manhattan. There he'd enjoy taking a Sunday stroll, sometimes picking through the trash outside Park Ave apartments in search of a treasure.

Morris set up his apartment just as it was in the Bronx, packed with framed photos and family heirlooms. Each knick-knack had a story which he shared with passion and in loving detail.

He was the docent of his own museum. Not only did my siblings and I continue to thoroughly enjoy our visits but a new generation, our children, got to absorb the history of our family as only he could tell it, oftentimes punctuated by readings from his diary.

For the last 20 years of his life, he would take his daily two-block walk to the Great Neck Senior Center where he became an institution. Each morning, he would put on his apron and serve the coffee. The price of a cup of coffee was 15 cents and a hug. He would drop the coins into a small container, step out from behind his serving table, and hold open his arms offering a loving, good morning hug. They called him "The Coffee Man." Like Morris, many of these seniors lived alone. For some, his hug was the only physical connection they had each day.

The Senior Center was housed in a closed elementary school and was shared by a daycare program. Many of the daycare youngsters were Spanish speakers, children of domestic workers in the upscale community. When needed, Morris would be called to the other side of the building to become the voice of the little ones, translating their needs into English. The children called him *'El viejito del café,'* the old man with the coffee.

Morris' last cup of coffee was served sometime after his 90th birthday. I was honored to give the eulogy at his funeral. As I surveyed the audience, I noted that our family only filled the first few rows. The rest of the room was overflowing with seniors from the Center deeply moved by his passing.

I saw many dabbing their eyes with their hankies, perhaps

wondering who would offer them a hug tomorrow. Or if ever there would ever be another "Coffee Man.'

French Jews were forced to wear this patch on their outer clothing.

Louie's Story

At eight, he looked like a puppet standing with the older kids at the one-room schoolhouse in Torgovitsa - a small town in Central Ukraine at the turn of the 20th century. It was rare to have a Jew in the Russian school. They usually got beat up and run off by the Russian boys. But there was something different about this child. He was quiet. Kept to himself. And he was brilliant.

Perhaps, it was his small size that kept him from being hit by the bigger Russian boys. He was very small for his age. They knew he would never fight back. They must have figured it wouldn't be much of a fight. More like beating a helpless puppy. Not a very manly exercise. So, they just left him alone.

Louie was the brightest boy in the Russian school. Recognized with year-end awards, he came home with Mark Twain's *'Tom Sawyer'* (in Russian) as a gift for his scholarship, a rare feat for a Jewish boy in that school. The book gave my grandfather his first taste of the world outside of his village.

Those were my grandfather Louie's early days. His father, David, briefly came to America in 1904 to avoid being drafted for the Russo-Japanese War. Jews rarely survived the Tzar's army. That made 7-year-old Louie the man of the house, head of the family, until his dad returned when the war ended.

In 1912, David, who we would call Zayda (Yiddish for Grandpa), set off with 15-year-old Louie to America to fulfill their American

Dream: a home on the Lower East Side of Manhattan. His wife Bessie and his four daughters were to follow a year later.

In December 1913, Bessie and the girls traveled Steerage Class on a ship named The Kursk. Three-year-old Malka, the youngest, died of appendicitis on board and was laid to rest in the frozen waters of the North Atlantic. Kaddish (the Jewish prayer for the dead) was chanted. Tears were shed. There is nothing sadder than the loss of a child.

Several days later, they arrived in New York harbor where the family was reunited in joyous laughter and gut-wrenching grief.

Zayda and Louie worked long hours stitching hats in the garment district. Louie quickly learned to speak and write English. Ten years later, he graduated from dental school and established a small practice. Over the next couple of years, three younger brothers were added to the family which now totaled nine. As the oldest son and best-established, Louie took on the role of head of the family. Zayda never learned to speak English.

In the late 1920s, he fell in love with a girl named Minnie. She was a firebrand, a garment district union organizer. He and my grandmother would eventually settle in an attached duplex on White Plains Road, a few doors in from the Westchester Avenue elevated train stop in the Bronx where they raised my mother and my uncle Jack. My grandfather's dental office was in the basement.

Building a dental practice was challenging in the middle of the Great Depression. For several years, to make ends meet, he became a dentist for the NYC police department. He was given a detective's badge, enabling him to ride the city's public transportation system for free. It must have been an odd sight to see my 5'4" grandfather with *The Forwards* (a Yiddish newspaper) folded under his arm as he flashed his NYPD detective's badge to enter the subway system.

Eventually, his practice could support his family. Like clockwork, each day at precisely 1:00 pm, he would come upstairs from the dental office to his favorite chair in the living room. Minnie would have a tuna fish sandwich and a piece of fruit set on a snack table in front of their boxy B&W television set. For over 30 years, he watched the CBS soap opera "As the World Turns," rarely missing an episode.

My grandfather placed a sugar cube on the inside of his cheek which dissolved when sipping his strong black tea, Russian style, often from a glass rather than a teacup. Even as they grew more affluent, a simple tea bag was reused for a second or sometimes a third serving.

The secret in our family was that my grandfather and my uncle Dave (his brother-in-law), would steal away for a few hours each Yom Kippur, the most solemn day in the Jewish year. But instead of atoning for their sins at morning services at Temple, they would ride the subway, a few stops to another neighborhood.... for their annual bacon and egg breakfast.

This bizarre act of defiance was so wrong on so many levels. Bacon is not kosher, and Jews are supposed to spend that day in Temple fasting. No doubt they popped Sen-Sen, powerful breath fresheners of the day - to neutralize the smell of bacon as they strolled in late to the Temple on the holiest day of the year.

My first home was a small apartment upstairs from my grandparents. My parents, my brother Andy and I lived there until we moved to Queens when I was three. We'd come back to the Bronx to visit my grandparents weekly until I went off to college.

When we were little, my brother and I liked to play in my grandfather's dental office. We would pump up his dental chair and make believe we were astronauts. The most fun we had was playing with the mercury he used to make dental fillings. Liquid mercury is very dense and shiny. It was mesmerizing pushing it around on the table, watching in amazement as it separated and then pulled together. It is also quite toxic and a wonder that we had not become horribly ill from the exposure.

Occasionally, a visit to their home in the Bronx included a dental checkup. My grandfather was a fine dentist, but he was not a big fan of novocaine (local anesthetic drug). So, while he drilled out my cavities - the result of my sugar laden diet - he would hum Bach cantatas. My fingers turned white gripping the arm rests of the dental chair. For years, I would cringe at the sound of a Bach cantata. Louie had the slowest drill imaginable.

My dad sarcastically referred to him as "Painless Louie."

After a dental appointment, we would grab a Bazooka bubble gum or some sticky candy from a large jar he had in his waiting room, thus, guaranteeing a return trip to hear him hum Bach once again.

Louie never forgot his community from Torgovitsa. As a young man, he was a founder and president of Torgovitsa Aid Society, a group dedicated to settling Jewish refugees from the Soviet Union. The Jews of Torgovitsa were exterminated by the Nazis during the Holocaust, but the Landsmen (those from the town) stayed close to each other and worked to free Soviet Jewry.

My grandfather tirelessly supported his siblings as they established their own families and he would take care of everyone's dental needs.

In the 1960s, he had a couple of heart attacks. In those days, the treatment was to stay home and rest. During these "time outs," Louie taught himself how to play the mandolin. He also became proficient on the concertina, an instrument similar to a small accordion. He inspired me to teach myself to play music which I have done my entire life.

Louie once took me to see the Mets at Shea Stadium. He needed to stop and place a nitroglycerin pill under his tongue as we trekked up the inclined walkway to our upper deck seats. He was no fan of baseball, but he loved me and how excited I got as I tried to explain the nuances of the game to him.

All he knew was Hank Greenberg, a Jew from the Bronx. He once came close to toppling Babe Ruth's single season home run record. When the game finally ended, I got up to stretch. He got up to leave.

I said this was a double header and that the second game would start shortly.

Always quick witted, he said "Oy vey iz mir! You brought me to a double headache?"

My grandfather rarely left the house without a jacket and tie. He dressed the way he thought a professional man should. On one of his weekly visits to our home in Queens, he came outside to watch me shoot baskets. The backboard and hoop were nailed to the front face of our garage. If I was home, that's where I'd be, practicing my jump shots, imagining I was playing for the Knicks at The Garden, a pudgy Jewish White boy with a better imagination than a jump shot.

"Nu? So, this is basketball? Mind if I try?" he said in his slight European/Bronx accent.

I set him up where the free throw line would be and handed him the ball. He unbuttoned his jacket and sunk five underhanded free throws in a row.

"Imagine I was a foot taller and forty years younger. Oy, such a game we would have. Now come in for dinner."

Louie and Zayda lived long lives, Louie into his 80's and Zayda nearly 100. Extraordinarily, my father, my grandfather, and my great grandfather all danced the Hora with me at my first wedding.

Dr. Louis Sissman and grandfather extraordinaire.

Bess And Dave

Sometime in the middle of the night she pulled on my big toe.

"We want in," she said.

Since they had been dead for forty years - I assumed that meant as a story in this book.

My aunt Bess and my uncle Dave have a wonderful story that deserves telling. So here goes:

The year was 1904. Bess, Rose, and my grandmother, Minnie were each under six when they came to America with my great grandmother, Ida. It was a harrowing trip from their small village in Russia, but no less dangerous than the increasing number of Pogroms that forced them to flee their home. With their earthly belongings stuffed in a couple of suitcases, they travelled through Europe to Liverpool where they booked Steerage class passage to New York.

Having no visible means of support, no husband, no job, no family, they were denied entry at Ellis Island and placed on the next steamer back to Liverpool. With dwindling funds, Ida immediately booked passage returning to the New World. This time Montreal where she found Canadians much more welcoming. From there, they made their way to the Lower East Side of New York, a 330-mile trip, the last leg of a very long journey.

Yes, I come from a family of illegal aliens. Frankly, I'm proud of it.

She and the girls settled into a three-room flat. Ida found work in the garment district, notorious for its hazardous sweat shops, and the girls started school.

Minnie, the oldest was an agitator. As a young woman, she was a union organizer, a Suffragette on a soap box making speeches, or marching for better wages, better working conditions. I got to know her as a sweet grey-haired grandma. I knew nothing of her extraordinary early life until well into my adult years.

Rose, the youngest sister was a bit "challenging." She was a tiny woman with a hair trigger temper. My earliest memory of her was my 5th birthday party. I blew out the candles before she got there.

"He blew out the candles. You didn't wait for me. Jesus Christ couldn't have gotten here any faster," she screamed at my mother and a house full of my 5-year-old friends.

She walked out and didn't speak with my parents again for months, even though she lived five blocks from us in Queens. Rose was a scary little woman who I stayed away from my entire life.

And then there was Bess. This story is about her. My uncle Dave you will get to know a bit later. Bess was the middle child, much taller than her sisters and the other Jewish immigrant girls in the Lower East Side. She was stunning. Statuesque. Bess was a good student. Excelled in math and science. Perhaps in another time, she would have become a professional woman, but these were the 1920s, between the wars. Pushcarts in the streets. Prohibition. Yiddish theater. Tenement living. And poverty. A time when young Jewish women were to be focused on learning how to make a good home, a kosher home, and to finding a good husband to share it with.

She had a lot of suitors. One young man named Nattie Birnbaum lived upstairs in her tenement building. They dated for a while, but there was no real "spark." She saw him perform in Vaudeville a couple of times - but didn't think he was very funny. Soon after, Nattie changed his name to George Burns. Yes, that George Burns, a comedian and national treasure.

Bess had a bit of a wild streak and was attracted to tough guys. When she met Dave, it was love at first sight. Simply put, Dave was a handful, but she knew she could tame him. Dave was one of the fighting Wallach brothers. All six of them had professional prize fights. Dave once told me that he was a much better lover than a fighter – "Getting punched in the face is no way to make a fucking living." His colorful language was a bit *harsh* for my 6-year-old ears.

His older brother, while in dental school, fought under an assumed name, Leach Cross......so their father wouldn't know he was a fighter. Leach fought for the lightweight crown in 1913 but lost. After more than 100 professional fights, he retired. He was known as "The Fighting Dentist." He once knocked another fighter's teeth out only to treat him the next day in his dental office. I met him when I was about five years old. At the time, I thought it odd that he was one of the best boxers in the world, yet he was so much smaller than my father, a NYC cop.

Dave gave up his boxing career but stayed close to the 'fight game' which had many colorful characters. Gangsters and such. He and his Jewish gang once sold barrels of watery bathtub gin during Prohibition. The Italian gangsters closed the deal paying them with counterfeit bills. Each walked away thinking they got the best of the other. The affair ended with laughter instead of bullets and a story they told for decades, becoming more colorful with each telling.

Dave was a terrible investor. The joke in my family was that if you wanted to make money in the market, you simply bought whatever stock he sold.

Dave once owned some land in the northeast Bronx. He thought it was worthless and sold it at a loss. It would later become a part of Co-Op City, at that time the largest housing cooperative in the world.

But Dave was happy-go-lucky. Content to be a garment cutter, he and Bess lived in a 4-story apartment building, a short walk to

Yankee Stadium. They had a sizeable apartment, large enough for my brother Andy and I to play hide and seek in.

The best hiding spot was my aunt's closet full of previously living creatures. Furs, a status symbol in the crowd they ran with. One of the furs was a fox stole, face and feet attached. That freaked us out. We used to chase each other around their apartment with it.

Andy and I would take turns riding the dumbwaiter, a small lift or freight elevator built to carry food from the ground floor to the apartment building's kitchens. We would take turns riding between her kitchen and her upstairs neighbor, Fanny. She would give us a hard candy each time we passed through. It was great fun. And incredibly dangerous.

But those were the 1950s when everyone smoked, cars had no seatbelts, and children played in the streets. And in dumbwaiters.

Bess was extraordinarily bright. She built her own television set from plans in *Popular Mechanics*. Each day, she would read *NY Times* cover to cover and complete the daily crossword puzzle. Fast. And in pen. She also took adult education classes, becoming fluent in Spanish.

Bess and Dave had a regular poker game with their friends in the building. The weekly game went on for decades. In their 70's they relocated the game to Miami Beach where they and their friends took apartments in the same complex off of Collins Ave.

Bess taught Andy and me how to play poker. I was six, Andy a few years older. Once we had the basics down, she taught us how to bet, bluff, and figure out what everyone was holding based on how they bet. She was a woman of endless patience except when it came to cards. When we were too slow to call the bet, she'd say, "Come on kid. Shit or get off the pot." I did say I was six, didn't I? God, I loved that woman.

Dave died when I was in college. I would call Bess at her retirement home. I had become a fairly good poker player making a part-time living from more affluent students. She giggled like a schoolgirl as

I described how I grabbed a big pot, bluffing with nothing more than a pair of 3s.

"Just like I taught you, kiddo," she laughed with pride.

Our conversation would be interrupted with her yelling at the Mets poor play on the television with the volume up. Too high. She never missed an inning in her old age.

I once visited Bess and Dave at their apartment on Miami Beach. They were well over eighty then. After lunch, Dave got up and put on a frilly apron. He cleared the table and started on the dishes.

"What's a matter, kid? You never saw a man do dishes?" he said. "That macho stuff is bullshit. I do the dishes. Then I can fool around with her tonight."

Bess blushed.

Dave and Bess with my father, Harold.

Harold

Calvin Coolidge. Prohibition. Flapper skirts. Babe Ruth. It was the time between the wars. The roaring twenties. A world full of promise and invention.

It was when my father was born in 1923 to immigrant parents in a four-story, cold-water walk up on the Lower East Side of NY. He was the youngest of four, a mid-life surprise to his Yiddish-speaking parents. His siblings were more than a dozen years older.

Growing up in that place at that time was rough. My dad had lots of fights. He got tossed out of Hebrew school and he quit high school in his junior year.

His older brother Morris recounted in his diary at the time that my dad would probably end up a gangster.

Eventually, he found his way out of the neighborhood to The Kings Point Merchant Marine Academy. In his white uniform, he had a fresh start, leaving behind the stench and violence of the Lower East Side.

There was an urgent need for Merchant seamen as the war was beginning in Europe. For the next 18 months, he sailed merchant ships to Europe, bringing critical supplies to Russia for them to fend off the Nazi invasion. Dad was awarded a medal by the Russian government for his heroic service, part of the famous "Forgotten Convoy" to Murmansk.

But one winter above the arctic circle was enough. He was itching to get into the fight and joined the Navy, enlisting as a Lieutenant - 2nd in command of a Navy Destroyer at the Invasion of Normandy. He was not yet 21 years old.

For his service, he was awarded the Legion of Honor Medal by the French Government in ceremonies in Paris and at Normandy on the 65th anniversary of the D-Day invasion. Along with my brother Andy and my wife, Norma, we accompanied him to France for this great honor, a highlight of our lives.

After the war, my father wanted to go to Israel to fight for the new Jewish homeland, but he fell in love with a girl named Betty and within a few short years, they were living in a 2-room apartment upstairs from my grandparent's attached home in the Bronx. That's where Andy and I were born.

He walked a beat as a NYPD patrolman, but he wasn't like other cops. His first partner was a Black patrolman. No one was quick to ride with a Black cop. Or a Jewish cop. So, they paired them together and they became friends. This was the early 1950's. Much of New York City was segregated.

Hitting the books never came easy to my dad, but he studied hard, passing the Civil Service Exam to become a Sergeant. My parents moved from the Bronx to a small home in Queens where Amy and then Tom came along. We were a family of six. My father was happy.

He had his home and his family in a safe neighborhood, far from the ugly streets he fought to get away from. He would spend countless evenings studying for his next Civil Service Exam. Soon he became a Lieutenant.

A few years later, he took and passed the Captain's exam, becoming one of the very few Jewish Captains in the New York City Police Department.

The NYPD was quick to identify my dad's unique ability to communicate with diverse groups of people often hostile to each other. With his calming demeanor, he could settle people down and keep the peace.

This was the late 1960s in the middle of the anti-war and civil rights movements. Amidst a backdrop of urban rioting and gang violence, he was promoted into Community Relations. There he thrived until he retired from the police force.

His fondest memories were his days in our Queens neighborhood of Cambria Heights, walking with his family to High Holy Day services at Temple Torah.

Temple Torah was an odd place of worship. Housed in a storefront on Linden Blvd, once the home of a small hardware store, the sanctuary was never quite completed. Folding chairs were placed beneath exposed electrical wires. Something was always broken, always being repaired, repainted, or retrofitted.

This was a small, tight-knit congregation with very little money. We could only afford part-time student Rabbis. Once in the mid-1960s, we had a Rabbi who was an anti-war leftist, more like a communist. His sermons and discussions made going to synagogue a loud and boisterous experience. It was chaos and my dad loved being in the middle of it.

My dad often misspoke. When my sister Amy left for college, he wanted to send her off with encouraging words. Saying for her to have a ball was not a big enough statement. He said, "Have many balls in college, doll."

On my parent's 15th wedding anniversary, he brought home a cake with the words "Fifteen Long Years" written on it. I was not yet 10 and even I knew he screwed that one up.

He was never one quick with a joke, but occasionally, he did say something completely odd and memorable.

I was about 16 and pretty full of myself. We were slap boxing. My hands were quicker than his, landing light slaps on his face as my feet moved like in Ali-like fashion. I stupidly uttered some street language.

"Come on, mother fucker. Let's see what you got."

In the moments that followed, I saw my life pass before my eyes with a certainty that he was about to put me through a wall. In that same moment, he pondered spending the rest of his life in prison for killing his obnoxious son. He took a beat and said, "You're damn right I'm a mother fucker or you wouldn't be here."

I exhaled. Happy to be alive.

Sometime after his 90th year, I asked him:

"Dad, when do you stop worrying about your children?"

He said, "I'll let you know."

He was a man of few words. But they were good words.

My Dad was proud to be a Jew. For him it was not religious. It was a tribal thing. Over the years, we'd call with news of the events of our lives. He would ask, tongue in cheek, "Is it good for the Jews?" He also loved to be at the head of the table for a Passover Seder. But he was also an Atheist.

That sounds incongruous, but that is who my father was, a very hard guy to pigeonhole or to label.

He was a Jew. But he was also an Atheist.

He was a NYC cop who earned the respect of both the Yippies and the Black Panthers.

He loved music but his choices were odd: Klezmer and Scottish Bag Pipes which he played loudly on his stereo, too early on a Sunday morning often pissing off my sleeping mother.

He loved to cook, but he was terrible at it. His culinary skills could best be summed up in two words: Tuna Burger.

He was a Navy man who couldn't swim. The only times he ever floated was in the Dead Sea and on my waterbed.

He was a high school dropout, but he possessed a master's level comprehension of 20th century European History. He was very,

very well read with a library of many hundreds of books.

He and my mother traveled the world, happily getting lost in places like Beijing, Jerusalem, Athens. Places where street signs were squiggles or fraternity letters. They didn't care. Rather than tours, they preferred taking local buses, finding their way around, meeting local people.

He was a war hero who hated war. He never talked about his own service during WWII. He was tough guy but had enough self-confidence to teach his grandson how to skip, enabling Amy's son, Justin to graduate from kindergarten.

He was a man who never sat his children down to a lecture. My dad was no Ward Cleaver. His wisdom was imparted by the way he lived his life. He taught by example.

He was a man who was uncomfortable with tender words. He rarely used the word love, but when my mother was in the last weeks of her life, he sat by her bedside singing songs from the life they had shared. Even the most hardened nurses on the hospital's Palliative Care wing at North Shore Hospital were moved to tears.

That is how he taught us about life. And about love.

My dad in Paris having just received the French Medal of Honor for his participation in the D-Day Invasion.

Acknowledgments

There are many people I would like to thank for helping me to create this book. My siblings, Andy, Amy, and Tom who have been in my life the longest helped me to remember the small details of the childhood we shared. My wife Norma, who gently pushed me to continue to write each time I thought I was done. Geno Paesano, my dear friend of four decades who helped me to polish and edit, but mostly to remind me that a good story is like the ads we used to write. They don't work without a good hook. Lastly, this book would not have happened without the friendship and support of Vangella Buchanan of The Writery Ink, LLC in Bloomfield, CT, who guided me through the publishing process.

Finally, a word to my children - Jason, Jonathan, Alexandra and Drew, and to my grandchildren – Emerson, Grant, Zoe and Juno. I wrote this book with thoughts of you. You should know the stories of the life and times of those who came before you. I did my best to convey these with honesty and humor. If any of my stories caused you discomfort or embarrassment, get over it. Life is sweet, but it is also messy. A little like eating Jell-O with your hands.

On the day of my high school graduation with my parents (Betty and Harold), grandparents (Louie and Minnie) and my siblings, Andy, Amy and Tom (in front)

Made in the USA
Middletown, DE
16 May 2022

65726191R00097